Notes on the Preparation of Essays in the Arts and Sciences

Fifth Edition

Revised and edited by

Mary Ann Armstrong
Martin Boyne
Maged El Komos
Karen Taylor

The Academic Skills Centre
at
Trent University
Peterborough, Ontairo
Canada K9J 7B8

2001

Notes on the Preparation of Essays in the Arts and Sciences

Printed by Richard's Printing,
Port Hope, Ontario, Canada

Fifth edition, 2001, reprinted 2004

National Library of Canada Cataloguing in Publication Data

Main entry under title:
       Notes on the preparation of essays in the arts and sciences

5th. ed.
Revised and edited by Mary Ann Armstrong, Martin Boyne,
Maged El Komos, and Karen Taylor
Includes index.
ISBN 1-894674-16-2

   1. Report writing. 2. English—Rhetoric. I. Armstrong, Mary Ann
II. Trent University. Academic Skills Centre III. Title.

LB2369.N68 2001   808'.042   C2001-900914-3

Published by the Academic Skills Centre at Trent University,
Peterborough, Ontario, Canada, K9J 7B8

Dedication

This book is dedicated to the writers of its earlier editions, who set the standards that the writers of the present edition have attempted to meet.

Peter Slade

Annette Tromly

Richard Harrison

Lucille Strath

Heather Avery

Isabel Henniger

Sheree-Lee Powsey

Kari Lie

Linda Zernask

CONTENTS

B. Methods of Documentation

C. Preferred Documentation Methods by
Academic Discipline

PREFACE

The launch of the fifth edition of *Notes* combines what has made previous editions so popular and useful with some refinements and necessary additions to bring the book into the twenty-first century. Much has changed in the eight years since the release of the fourth edition in 1993, the most significant being, of course, the proliferation of electronic research sources both on the Internet and in other media. Only quite recently have the major documentation styles standardized their guidelines for electronic and online citation methods; this edition of *Notes* reflects these standards while acknowledging the need for flexibility during a period of ongoing (but exciting) change in the way research is conducted by scholars.

Consequently, the principal addition to the book in its latest incarnation is a section on documenting online sources in all of the major styles: footnoting/endnoting, MLA, APA, and CBE. In addition, examples have been updated and explanations streamlined and clarified in response to the feedback of the primary users of the book: students. It is thanks to them–and to their instructors–that *Notes* continues to be a required or highly recommended research companion in schools, colleges, and universities across Canada and beyond our borders.

Part I, Preparation, has been revised to provide readers with a concise introduction to the fundamentals of essay writing. *Thinking It Through*, our guide to academic essay writing, continues to be the best source for detailed information on the topic, in conjunction with our shorter publications on specific skills. A notable addition to Part I, however, is a useful section on conducting internet research, with a focus on the evaluation of web documents. Despite the practicality and convenience of online research, pitfalls abound; this new section directs students to avoid such problem areas and conduct effective online research by following valuable tips on assessing the credibility, authorship, and purpose of web documents.

Part II, Format, remains relatively unchanged but has been updated to reflect the reality that most essays are now prepared on word processors, which can be instructed to format most aspects of the essay manuscript, such as page numbering and footnotes, automatically. This section is still valuable for guidelines on capitalization, italicization, and writing numbers and units of measurement.

Part III, Documentation, is the core of the book. A useful first section provides guidance on the practical aspects of documenting, from the proper use of primary and secondary sources to the difference between paraphrasing and quoting directly. This introduction prepares students for the mechanics of referencing in the Methods of Documentation section, which deals in turn with footnoting and endoting, parenthetical documentation in both MLA and APA styles, and the number-reference method. Part III has been updated in keeping with the official style guides produced by the MLA, APA, and CBE and includes, as mentioned, comprehensive treatment of online and other electronic sources.

The final section of Part III provides the preferred documentation styles by the academic disciplines taught at Trent and includes detailed examples and guidelines for all the major humanities, social science, and natural and physical science disciplines, along with sections on interdisciplinary studies. Most disciplines, as students soon discover, have idiosyncratic ways of adapting the principal documentation styles; this section is therefore invaluable for students as they aspire to conform to each discipline's expectations.

We hope that the new spiral-bound design for this fifth edition of *Notes* will make it an easier reference tool for the computer workstation. Long-time readers will also note that we have returned to the traditional green cover after an accidental experiment with white for the fourth edition. Green, we have found, is more impressive, especially since many readers still refer to it as "the green book." But whether the book is green or white, it is the contents that matter, and we hope that this new edition will live up to the excellent reputation that *Notes* has had since its humble origins almost three decades ago.

Acknowledgments

In addition to the dedication that appears on p. iii, we must express our gratitude to those who have more recently contributed to the publication of *Notes*. Students have come to depend on the book as their first reference source for documentation; similarly, we have come to depend on them for their comments on the book's readability and helpfulness.

Many of the changes stem directly from students' comments. Faculty at Trent University have also provided input for the discipline-specific section and for general improvements to the design and content.

At the Academic Skills Centre we are fortunate to have colleagues who are dedicated to the production of excellent publications. We must therefore thank the following instructors and support staff, past and present, for their ongoing contributions to the publications program, of which this book remains the flagship text: Deb Nichols, Ruth Brandow, Sheila Collett, Peggy Krüger, Kevin Spooner, Peter Lapp, Fausta Capogna, Tania Pattison, and Ellen Dempsey.

As writers and editors of this book we too have learned much and have been collectively driven toward greater accuracy, clarity, and precision in the process. This fifth edition is the product of a truly collaborative process of which we are proud to be part.

Mary Ann Armstrong
Martin Boyne
Maged El Komos
Karen Taylor

Peterborough,
July 2001

PART I: PREPARATION

Writing a university essay is a particular kind of learning, an experience students may or may not have encountered in their earlier education. What may be new to students is the expectation that the essay should be, above all, an exercise in thinking. **The essay is not meant to include everything a student knows about a topic or to catalogue pages of unassimilated information. Rather, its purpose is to examine and interpret a body of material.** In addition to describing a subject, such as an historical event or a repeated image in a poem, the essay will usually examine the *why* and *how* of the subject. In an essay, the material is analysed; the writer finds a means by which to account for the evidence examined and, in doing so, makes this evidence coherent and logical. An essay may, for instance, isolate the cause of an historical event, or it may explain the function of a poetic image. In short, the essay gives students a chance to show, not merely that they have acquired information, but that they can reflect upon and learn from this information and use it to advance or defend a claim.

As the next few pages indicate, essay writing involves a number of stages, stages which are treated here as separate and distinct steps in a process. **It is important to remember, though, that the process is never simple, and that it is always fluid; the stages merge and separate, expand and contract, depending upon the nature of the material being treated.** Even the most methodical writers will change their procedures somewhat with every essay. And many writers depart from set patterns as they become more experienced in writing essays and as they develop their own styles. The scheme described here for the preparation of essays is meant to be a flexible guideline, not a prescriptive set of rules. For those students who are either learning essay-writing skills for the first time or facing especially stubborn materials, the method will offer direction and, we hope, encouragement.

Planning the Essay

From Topic to Thesis

Essay assignments come in many different forms. Sometimes — especially in upper-year courses — the topic is left entirely to the student. Sometimes an instructor designates a broad subject area which the student will need to narrow to a manageable size. And sometimes a more focused essay topic is assigned — perhaps in the form of a question, a problem to solve, a statement to evaluate, or a quotation to discuss. Regardless of the form your topic takes, the process of writing an essay involves moving from a general understanding of the topic to a clear presentation of a *position* on that topic which will be your thesis or controlling idea.

The process begins with a question; even if your topic does not ask a question, you should decide on one that you want your essay to investigate. You can do this by thinking about the topic you have. Look to your reading on the subject, your ideas, your lectures, and your conversations with others. When you discover a central problem or question related to your topic, you have completed the first step in developing a thesis. The thesis is not the question but the answer to your central question, indicating both what the essay will address and how your analysis will proceed. In writing an essay, then, you will be making clear your answer and supporting it. But the essay is never the final word. It is written to say, "This is the conclusion to which my thinking and reading to date have brought me."

The exact time at which you develop your thesis will vary from essay to essay. You should be thinking toward a thesis even during the earliest stages of research. Many students develop a thesis by writing a first draft; doing so allows them to explore, think through, and clarify their central concern or inquiry on paper. They can then look back over what they have written to discover their line of thought and impose whatever organization or structure on it that is necessary. This is a perfectly valid way to work; but remember, if this is your method, your first draft will probably require extensive revision and editing. Of course, you cannot arrive at a final thesis until you have completed your research — you do not know the answer yet! — but giving some thought to a thesis at an early stage will help you direct your research efforts.

Moreover, an appropriate thesis is key to a good essay. Keep in mind that the thesis of your essay should never be self-evident: "Charles Darwin is associated with evolution" is not a thesis. The thesis is a position or perspective, defended or explained by a carefully planned structure of ideas and supported by evidence. On the other hand, it need not be controversial. "Charles Darwin's ideas are outrageous" and "Charles Darwin's *Origin Of Species* was the first coherent expression of the theory of evolution" are both theses, but the former is a more extreme statement and therefore hard to justify.

Remember that the thesis of an essay is different from its topic; it goes beyond the topic to make an assertion. Usually, you will assert your thesis in what is called the thesis statement. If your topic, for example, is "Charles Darwin's contribution to knowledge," your thesis statement will make some sort of assertion about that topic. Figure 4 (pp.

14-15) shows the outline of an essay written on this topic with the following thesis statement: "Charles Darwin did not invent the theory of evolution. However, backed by careful observation, *Origin of Species* presented such a coherent expression of the theory that the burden of proof shifted from the supporters of evolution to those who denied its validity." The thesis statement, then, states what the essay is claiming and the method by which that claim will be explained and supported. It expresses, in a general but precise statement, the analytic purpose of the essay. It focuses your essay and coordinates and synthesizes your thinking, research, and writing. **Most often, the thesis statement will be brief — no more than a sentence or two. Usually, it will appear in a prominent place in your essay: often in the introductory paragraphs, but sometimes not until the conclusion.**

It is best to try to express your thesis in a single statement, but do not be alarmed if this seems impossible. Some essays do not lend themselves to such a compressed treatment of their main claim. A thesis which unfolds more gradually — perhaps through several separate points made throughout the essay — can also be effective. But remember that your reader must be clear about just what constitutes the essay's central assertion, and you must know your thesis *before* you start to write the final draft of your essay.

For many students, finding a thesis is the most difficult part of writing an essay. When you are having trouble coming up with a central idea, try making a planning sheet: list all the important and interesting ideas that have occurred to you about the topic in your reading and thinking, and see if you can find one that you want to emphasize or develop, or several that you want to relate in some way. If you are still undecided about a thesis, try discussing your ideas with a friend or classmate, or do some exploratory writing. Often just expressing your thoughts, either aloud or on paper, can help you discover a controlling idea with which you can begin work.

4

Figure 1: From Topic to Thesis

Topic	Questions (to think about)	Possible Theses
Darwin's Theory of Evolution	Well, what about it? Why do we learn about it? Why was it so important? Why was it so influential? Why did it become so influential?	Charles Darwin's ideas are outrageous. (*extreme and difficult to support*) Charles Darwin's *Origin of Species* was the first coherent expression of the theory of evolution. Charles Darwin's *Origin of Species* presented such a coherent expression of the theory of evolution that the burden of proof shifted from the supporters of evolution to those who denied it.

Researching the Essay

Not all essays require consulting dozens of books and articles. In an English course, for example, you may be asked to use only a play or a poem as your research material; your observations on the work and the argument you extract from these observations will constitute your entire essay. But all essays you write will require some form of research, of collecting information, in primary sources (public records, maps, statistics, poems or plays, etc.), secondary sources (articles, editorials, textbooks, etc.), or both. It is important to undertake the essay with a clear idea of how one goes about collecting this information.

Some students think of research as a fairly passive process that goes on prior to — and apart from — the planning of an essay. These students are likely to spend many wasted hours in the library, taking notes on a very broad (and sometimes vaguely defined) topic. They put off doing any directed thinking about the claims and structure of their essay until after their notes have accumulated. **The more efficient way to work is to plan the essay and do research at the same time.** Research is more than mere notetaking: it involves getting an overview of your topic, narrowing the topic, selecting the most useful sources or observations, thinking toward a thesis, and, finally, collecting information directed to a particular end.

Selecting Material

Once you have chosen a topic and rephrased it as a question or a tentative assertion, research should begin — and you must work actively. From the minute that you open a book, you are working not only to collect information but also to plan the essay and further define an appropriate thesis. Moreover, you also want to discover a way of considering your topic that permits you to write a paper of appropriate length in the time you have allotted. **As you work, write.** It is probably not advisable to take content notes as soon as you open a book, but it certainly is worthwhile to jot down ideas that strike you, play at rewording your thesis, sketch tentative outlines, or even draft a few paragraphs when a particular aspect of your paper becomes clear.

Researching usually proceeds most smoothly if you work to gain a general understanding of your topic before reading in detail about specifics. If you are using secondary sources, quickly reading or skimming one or two short but general works on your topic (books, articles, appropriate web sites) and looking at the tables of contents in other books on the subject will help you see what questions or controlling ideas might be fruitful.

Another useful step is to compile a working bibliography (a list of potentially useful books and articles). The online catalogue, bibliographies, indexes, and abstracts will help you; the reference librarian can show you how to use these tools. You can also conduct an internet search to find electronic sources which complement your print ones. Gather a wide selection of material for your working bibliography; remember, at this stage your final thesis is still undetermined, so it will be difficult to know exactly which works will ultimately be most useful to you. Once you have a working bibliography, check the table of contents and the index of each book you have to see how each work relates to your topic. Skim the introductory and concluding chapters (or the introductory and concluding paragraphs of articles), as well as the relevant sections of a source, to determine what the argument of each work is and to see how these various perspectives might affect your own thesis.

As you skim, you must evaluate. The date of publication will sometimes aid you in assessing the importance of a source. In some disciplines (for example, the sciences) you will need information that is up-to-date. In other disciplines you may not want the most recent works; in history, for instance, works contemporary with your subject may be particularly useful. Noting who wrote the book or article might help also. (Is the author well respected in the field? Do you recognize any biases?) Do not, however, aim simply to choose works which support one another; an essay that tries to come to grips with evidence that is contradictory or opinions that conflict will be superior to one that ignores problem areas.

Taking Notes

Once you have a rough idea of the material you need to read and can formulate a tentative thesis (and perhaps can recognize what the sections of your paper might be), you are ready to take content notes. Your thesis and outline can be revised and developed as you read, take notes, and write, but having them roughed out at this stage will give direction to your notetaking. Remember, the aim is not to gather a great mass of notes but to gather notes directed to a particular end. Keeping in mind the approximate length of each section of your paper will help you keep your notes brief and to the point; making decisions now about what is important enough to use, and therefore to note, will make the actual writing much easier.

At this stage, you should prepare a bibliographic note for every source consulted. There are certain standard pieces of information that are needed to complete any citation: author, title, and publication information. Consult the recommended documentation style for your discipline in Part III and see what information you will need to provide about each source. Doing so before taking content notes will ensure that you do not have to return to the library the day your essay is due to complete a list of works cited.

When you finally come to take content notes, **do not read books and articles slavishly from beginning to end. Read with a purpose — to find particular kinds of information**. Furthermore, read critically. Distinguish between fact and opinion, and when a writer puts a certain interpretation on a piece of evidence, ask yourself whether that is the only interpretation possible and whether other evidence supports the argument.

As for the notes themselves, they can take a variety of forms. Most of your notes will probably paraphrase information contained in a source; reformulating material in your own words at this point will improve your understanding and will make the writing of the essay easier. You may also choose to copy short passages, particularly from primary sources. Statistics you may simply record. Be careful, however, to distinguish in your notes between quoted and paraphrased material. It will be important when you write your essay to know what material needs merely a citation and what material is a quotation. See Part III-A for more on this.

You may make your notes either on file cards, on ordinary paper, or in electronic form. Web and other electronic sources allow you to copy to computer files where you can then add your own notes and comments. Be sure to record pertinent documentation. If you use file cards for notes, put only one fact or idea on each card. Later, when your outline is fully developed, you will be able to label each note to indicate where it belongs in the outline and to put the cards in the order in which the points should appear in the essay. Electronic notes can also be categorized and organized, but ensure that bibliographic notes do not get separated from content notes in this process. If you make your notes on paper, leave wide margins so that you can add your own comments or cross-refer to other notes. Taking notes on only one side of the page will permit cutting and pasting.

Internet Research

Evaluating Web Documents

Of course, researchers must evaluate any information source that they plan to use. When conducting web research, however, this evaluation is particularly important, and often tricky.

Web publications are not regulated or checked for accuracy. They do not have to be edited or approved by an organization, publisher, or

8

corporation. Besides, web publishing is not costly or time-consuming; it is open to anyone with sufficient funds to purchase internet access.

Because electronic documents can be easily and quickly revised at little additional cost to the author, they can change rapidly, making critical evaluation a difficult, ongoing task. In short, the relative ease and freedom of web publishing as compared with print publishing means that individuals from all walks of life and with many purposes and perspectives can have their say using the Web, and they can revise their opinions and expressions at will.

Much excellent information that would never otherwise be available is now made public on the Web — lecture notes, conference papers, and research reports, for example. Some web pages, however, are published as jokes or are intentionally misleading for less benign purposes. A commercial site, for example, might imitate the site of a famous professional organization in order to gain credibility and make sales.

Sometimes, special interest groups or even governments might attempt to pass their web pages off as belonging to a more objective party by disguising the web address (URL). Even web sites that seem to present scholarly, fair-minded information may be authored by well-meaning but uninformed amateurs lacking authority. And it is often difficult to determine who the author is and for what purpose the web site was created. In general, however, the same criteria that you use to evaluate print sources can be extended to web-site evaluation.

Publisher or Sponsor

Some web sites are sponsored by professional associations or societies such as the Canadian Bar Association; by universities, museums, libraries, or research centres; or by newspapers, broadcasting companies, or print publishers. These sites are often as reliable as print sources because their sponsors have to maintain a reputation for truthful, accurate scholarship or reporting. Always consider whether a web page is being published by an individual purchasing space on the Web or whether it is being sponsored, and by whom.

Author/Authority

A web site or page that gives considerable information about its author and his or her credentials is usually more trustworthy than one providing only an e-mail address or no information about authorship. Still, giving

Figure 2: Tips for the Internet Researcher

Bookmark Internet Documents: Doing this will ensure that you can find all the web documents you have used in your paper. It will also help you to cite each URL (address) correctly.

Copy & Paste URLs: If you use your word-processor to copy and paste web addresses directly into your bibliography or list of references, there is less chance of making a typing error. Beware, however, of web sites that use frames; sometimes the URL in your browser's window is **not** the address of the document you are viewing in a frame.

Print Significant Web Documents: Doing this gives you a permanent record of your research, which is useful considering the speed at which internet documents and addresses change. Also, printing at least the first page of a web site can give you an easily accessible record of the bibliographic information you will need for an internet citation: the URL, title, author's name, and the date on which you accessed the site. (Remember that the page numbers of your printout may not be the same as those on other people's, so do not use these numbers in your citations.)

Use Creative Search Techniques: Often, even recently cited internet documents will be difficult to find on the Web. Perhaps a portion of a web address has changed, which means that you get an error message such as "unable to locate the server." If you eliminate portions of the old URL, progressing from the back to the front, you might still discover where an internet provider now hosts the page you once found. (Note: This technique also helps you discover the authors and hosts of internet documents when this information is not presented on a web page.)

Figure 3: Internet Citation Checklist

- **Do I have the correct and complete URL?**

- **Do I know whom to credit for this site?** Have I noted the complete name or names of all of the authors? Is there a corporate or government author or sponsor? Have I noted this information?

- **Do I have all the title information I need?** It is often necessary to refer to specific sections of web documents, so you might need to record sub-headings as well as the titles of articles, of journals, of short stories that are part of a large web site, and of the major internet document or site.

- **Did I record when the page was created and last updated?** It is useful to note all the information available regarding date of publication, edition, and last revision.

- **Did I note when I accessed the document?**

- **Have I evaluated the web source?** What are the credentials of its authors and sponsors? Does my other research support the evidence presented on the Web?

- **Have I printed out the important parts of the web documents that I plan to use?** We suggest printing out at least the first page of an important web source in order to have printed evidence of both the information you need to document this source and the contents of a web page on the day you viewed it.

- **Have you checked the URL recently?** A good policy is to check, right before you hand in your paper, that the web documents you refer to still exist and have not changed their addresses.

false credentials and a pseudonym is a possibility, so do some research on the author to try to verify biographical statements made on web pages. Perhaps, if all else fails, you could consider contacting the author by e-mail, if an address is provided. Although your questions to the author should be diplomatic, your main intention is to establish the author's qualifications for publishing on the topic of the web site or page. Is the author an authority, an expert in this field?

Date of Publication/Date of Last Revision
Some web pages are "ghosts," floating in cyberspace abandoned by their creators. These pages will either have no dates on them anywhere — readers can't tell when they were first created or last updated — or the date of their last revision will be in the distant past (over a year ago in cybertime). A more reliable internet document will list the date on which it was last revised, at the very least. Some list the dates of all versions, and these are probably the most reliable. Outside of decisions regarding whether or not to trust a web document, currency is still an issue. Check that the information on any web page you find is current enough to be useful to you.

Evidence/Other Links and References
Does the web site provide references to other print and electronic resources? Does it list appropriate and active links to relevant web pages on the topic? A trustworthy site will offer support for its claims in the form of verifiable citations of print and electronic sources.

Accuracy and Bias
You need to use all the knowledge you have to assess the accuracy and perspective of a web source. Consider whether there are small mistakes, typographical errors, wrong dates, misspelled words or names. Compare the internet document to others, both print and electronic, especially to those written for different purposes or expressing alternative views. Examine the content. Does it seem reasonable and logical? Does it represent other perspectives and sources fairly? Look at the style of writing. A reliable source will tend to use formal, objective language and avoid slang and hyperbole.

Purpose/What are you Selling?
Some web pages are nothing more than infomercials whose purpose is to sell you a service or product. These may play fast and loose with the truth.

Others aim to propagate particular views, ideas, doctrines, or policies. These may or may not respect the ethic of objective analysis. The most reliable are internet documents whose purpose is to publish scholarship and research. It is as important to determine the purpose of a web site as its authorship.

Reviews and Awards
Sometimes, a web site will list awards it has received or links to positive reviews. Teachers, librarians, and other information specialists regularly review new sites, and many professional societies grant awards to the web sites that their members find the most useful and authoritative. These reviews and awards can help to guide you to good internet documents. Reviews also provide excellent examples of the process of evaluating web resources.

Consult Figures 2 and 3 for at-a-glance information on accurate and efficient citation from the Internet and other electronic sources.

Organizing The Essay

Once you have established your thesis and have some grasp of your research material, you can concentrate on organization to make sure that all the sections will work together to validate your main idea. An **outline** provides a good opportunity for exploring how the essay will be organized, and the best kind of outline is one that helps you develop your thesis. Often you will find that the thesis statement suggests its own organizing principles: the main steps by which you establish your argument or validate your thesis will become the main sections and subsections of your essay. Regardless, everything in your outline should be relevant to the central assertion you have chosen. This is why single-word headings in outlines are not useful; you need instead to use statements that focus your thought. In this way, the outline will allow you to refine your thinking about your argument. When you see your argument as a physical picture on a page, you will be able to determine more easily what should be emphasized, what should be of greater, equal, or subordinate importance, what should be deleted, what should be expanded, and what should be rearranged.

As you draw your outline, pay careful attention to the structure of assertions and evidence in your plan. Remember that you are trying to show your reader the validity of your thesis through the careful use of supporting material. Figure 4 shows an outline for an essay with a fairly complicated thesis. Like the thesis in this example, your thesis statement should be adequately developed through several major and supporting points into which you have divided your thesis for analysis. Under each point will be evidence relevant to that particular idea.

During the writing stage, almost everyone discovers new things to say, new ideas, or new arrangements of ideas. If you have at least a basis from which to work, and to which you can return if the new ideas do not turn out to be helpful, you can more readily explore lines of argument. Not having an outline, on the other hand, either through not giving yourself time to organize your ideas properly or through neglecting to make a plan, means that you are writing the essay "out of your head" and may only be unpacking the contents of your mind onto the page in an unorganized way.

Sometimes and for some writers, however, preparing an outline in advance of drafting is very difficult. When this is the case, a very quick rough draft may be the best way to begin writing. From the rough draft, an outline should emerge, and from the outline the writer can prepare a second, more organized version of the essay.

Writing the Essay

Even a well-planned essay can be difficult to begin. If it is, the main thing to do is to start writing. Once you have broken through your initial resistance and have begun to fill the blank space in front of you, ideas will begin to flow. Your first draft, after all, is not what you will submit; consider it as a rough effort — something you will be able to revise later — and the void may seem less forbidding.

The First Draft
The most carefully planned essay will always require further thinking during the writing stage. Indeed, in the act of writing you will often discover ideas or clarify thoughts; you can write to find out what you think. You can write to discover your thesis, or, if you have established your basic plan, you can merely sketch a rough draft fairly quickly,

Figure 4: A Sample Outline

THESIS — Charles Darwin did not invent the theory of evolution. However, backed by careful observation, *Origin of Species* presented such a coherent expression of the theory that the burden of proof shifted from the supporters of evolution to those who denied it.

Major Point I. Evolutionary theory was not new; it was, before Darwin, part of the history of biology.

supporting point A. There were other evolutionary theorists.

evidence 1. Aristotle
2. Erasmus Darwin

supporting point B. Darwin's debt to these thinkers

evidence 1. Darwin's own acknowledgement
2. Huxley on Darwin

Major Point II. Darwin's observations were thorough. They made the notions of adaptation and selection plausible.

supporting point A. The relationship between structure and function in finches' beaks

Figure 4, continued

supporting point	B.	How selective breeding produced "better" domestic animals
Major Point	III.	If those who wrote after *Origin of Species* wanted to deny evolution, they had to develop better explanations for evidence they all acknowledged.
evidence		1. Religious opponents
evidence		2. Scientific opponents

while the ideas are still fresh. At the earliest stages of writing, exact expression is less important than inquiry and overall shaping. Concentrate first on getting your ideas down on paper; allow time for revision later.

Many people find that the introduction and the conclusion are the most difficult parts of the essay to write. Remember that you need not begin your rough draft at the beginning; often introductions can be more effectively written after other sections of the draft have been completed. Instead of trying to compose a graceful and eloquent introduction immediately, just write down your thesis and then start to develop one of the first major points in your outline.

In general, the beginning of an essay has two purposes: to capture the reader's interest and to introduce your material. Avoid beginnings which are too general, too theoretical, or too far removed from the essay's central concerns. When concluding, you should manage to avoid two extremes. On the one hand, do not write a conclusion which restates your argument in exactly the same words you have used throughout the essay; such repetition provides only a mechanical ending, which will not be interesting to your reader. (It is important, though, to remind your reader of your thesis in the conclusion.) On the other hand, be careful not to introduce entirely new ideas in your final paragraph; your reader will be frustrated if the essay suddenly presents unresolved issues. One useful compromise between these two extremes might be to widen the

16

perspective on your subject somewhat by suggesting how it has implications beyond the ones with which you have dealt.

Revising and Proofreading

After you have written your essay in a rough form, pay close attention to revising the draft. Adopt a method for revising systematically. One useful scheme is to **read a hard copy draft several times, paying attention to one aspect of the essay (content, organization, use of language, mechanics) at a time.**

It is probably best to pay attention to **organization** first. Your task at this level of revision is to create a structure that will help your reader see how all the segments of the paper relate to your main thesis. Using your outline as a guide, check your draft to ensure that you have composed sentences which articulate the major point of each section and its relation to the main thesis. Then, ensure that in the paragraphs of each section the relationship of each paragraph to the major point is clear. Remember that ideas relate in very precise ways; one part of your essay can exemplify, contradict, expand, or qualify another. Linking words (such as "however," "nevertheless," "therefore," "conversely") can help you clarify for your reader the logical connections between thoughts.

Within paragraphs, use transitional devices such as linking words, repetition of key terms, and pronouns so that the reader can see easily how an idea is being developed. Keep in mind that a paragraph shorter than three sentences generally does not develop an idea fully and that a paragraph longer than a double-spaced typewritten page (300 words) may be difficult for a reader to follow.

Even the smallest unit in your essay — the individual word — will require careful thought at some stage of revision. Subtle differences in meaning can make one word considerably more appropriate than another. Consult a good dictionary; it can help you distinguish words from one another and find alternative and more precise ways to express your thoughts. Be aware also of the difference between denotations (dictionary meanings) and connotations (associations attaching to the word). The dictionary might define green as a colour, but this word has also come to be associated connotatively with environmental protection. Finally, remember that the context in which a word is used can affect its appropriateness. The word "interface," for instance, has a precise meaning in the field of computer science, but in other disciplines it might be no more than vague and empty jargon. During the final stages of revision, pay careful attention to matters of expression. Have you in every case chosen the clearest phrasing, the most appropriate language, and the most precise words to convey your ideas?

Proofreading — the final stage of essay preparation — should not be forgotten. Putting the best face on your essay, by submitting a clear copy with ample margins and careful spelling, is certain to make a difference. Many mistakes in writing, typing, grammar, or spelling can be picked up by reading your draft aloud at least once. While spell and grammar checkers can be useful, they do not eliminate the need for you to proofread for mistakes yourself. Spell-check will not identify a word you have spelled incorrectly if your mistake happens to be a valid word itself. If you misspell *it's* as *its*, or *there* as *their*, spell-check will not recognize the error. Grammar-check has limited usefulness as well. A grammar-check can point out possible errors, but it is not much help to have pointed out to you, for example, that your sentence lacks pronoun-antecedent agreement, if you have no idea what that means or how best to fix it. The checkers' analysis of your prose can be inaccurate, and you should have the ability to assess their advice and decide whether to follow it or not. Both tools can be of some help, but you are still mainly responsible for the clearness and correctness of your writing.

In the final stage of preparation, the title page and documentation sections will also need your attention. Choose a title that reflects fairly specifically what your essay is about; overly clever, vague, or cryptic titles will only confuse your reader. For rules of documentation, see Part III.

Style
As you turn your attention to the style of your essay, remember that you have two responsibilities: one to your reader and one to your material. For your reader you must make your ideas as accessible as possible. **Use language that is precise and direct**. Always choose the most straightforward means of expression. This is not to say, however, that you should write using only simple, short words and sentences. Thoughtful ideas and explanations may well require complex sentence structures and a good vocabulary. Your second responsibility, indeed, is to the material of your essay, and your style must do justice to its complexity. Choose words that express accurately and completely what you mean to say, constructions that establish what is emphatic or subordinate in your thinking, and transitions that clarify exactly how one thought relates to another. If you find yourself writing vaguely, and revisions seem inadequate, check to see if your words, particularly words that are key to

your essay, reflect clearly what you are trying to say. Focus on a problem word or passage and ask yourself what its meaning is. Search for words that more accurately express that meaning.

Language that is simple and precise is suitable for an essay in any academic discipline. Certain small stylistic practices, however, may be encouraged by some departments and discouraged by others. For instance, it was generally the practice in the past to use the third person ("the researcher" or "one") when making reference to oneself in a scientific paper. The reasoning behind this practice was that the writer should be separate or detached from the argument presented. It is still the case that in a scientific experiment the passive voice rather than the active voice is used. When we use the passive voice, we write, "The solution was heated to 40 degrees C." When we use the active voice, we write, "I heated the solution to 40 degrees C." The sentence using the passive voice does not require the use of the first person, "I."

However, it is now more widely recognized that the conclusion that you are arguing in scientific papers is the result of your own thinking on the basis of the evidence that you have gathered. Therefore, the use of "I" is more widely accepted in science papers, as well as in social science and humanities papers, because it is recognized that the author's mind informs every word in the paper. You should, if you are in doubt about this practice, ask your instructor or consult a leading journal in your discipline.

As you encounter essay writing in a number of different courses, try to develop an awareness of particular demands. Different disciplines, materials, intended audiences, and purposes will force you to change your writing style slightly. With practice you will be able to adapt your individual style to changing expectations and tasks.

This brief introduction to essay writing may not answer all your questions. For more detailed instruction, you should consult our other Academic Skills Centre publications.

PART II: FORMAT

Preparation of the Essay Manuscript

1. Use white paper of standard size (8½ x 11 inches).
2. Type or print out the essay. Check with your professor before handing in a hand-written essay. Use a typeface that is similar to Times Roman or Courier and about 12 points in size.
3. Type or print on one side of the paper only.
4. Double-space the entire essay: text, quotations, and the Bibliography/Works Cited/Reference list. Leave margins of 1 inch at the top, bottom and both sides of the page so that the marker has room to make comments. Indent paragraphs 5 spaces from the left margin.
5. Number *all* pages, except the title page or the figures pages if you have them, with Arabic numerals (1, 2, 3, etc.) in the top right-hand corner. Do not use an abbreviation before the page number. Do not use a period, bracket, or any other punctuation mark after the page number. You may include your last name before each page number (Jones 3).
6. You may include a separate title page which clearly indicates your name, the date, the title of the essay, and the name and number of the course (e.g., History 100), *or* you may type your name, your professor's name, the course name, and the date in the upper left margin of your essay's first page. Double-space after this information, centre the title, and double-space again before beginning the essay text. Check with your instructor that this second method is acceptable.
7. Staple or clip pages together at the top left-hand corner. Submit essays unfolded unless your professor indicates otherwise. Do not bind the essay into a folder unless requested to do so.
8. Some disciplines permit, or even encourage, the use of headings and subheadings to indicate sections of the essay. Check with your professor.
9. Consult a reputable Canadian, British, or American dictionary for acceptable spelling. Choose one system of spelling and use it consistently throughout the essay.

Abbreviations

Abbreviations and acronyms are most commonly used when documenting source material.

Sometimes, however, they are used in the text of an essay or research paper. When deciding whether to use an abbreviation or acronym, consider the reader. If your reader will be more familiar with the abbreviation than with the complete form it represents, use the abbreviation. Some examples might be CBC, DNA, IQ, NATO, OPEC, REM, Rh, and UNESCO. If, on the other hand, there is the slightest possibility that your reader will be confused by the abbreviation, consider not using it. Would spelling out the term throughout the paper be a nuisance? If you decide that you do want to use an abbreviation, for reasons of economy, even though your reader might be puzzled by it, spell the term out completely the first time, following this with the abbreviation in parentheses: General Agreement on Tariffs and Trade (GATT). Whatever you decide, be consistent throughout the paper, and, should you use abbreviations, use conventional forms. Any good general dictionary will list conventional abbreviations. Appendix 1 contains a list of the abbreviated forms of the provinces, territories, and states of Canada and the United States. These abbreviations should be used in documentation when the place of publication is not well known.

Capitalization

Most English speakers are familiar with basic capitalization rules: people's names are capitalized, as are the names of places and the letters beginning sentences. In academic writing, however, it is often useful to know a few of the more intricate rules governing capitalization.

1. **Proper Nouns**

   All proper nouns, which are nouns that name specific persons, places, and things, are capitalized. Proper nouns include, but are not limited to, the following: names of people (and their titles) and places; names of government departments, political parties, and organizations; names of institutions; names of nationalities and languages; names of races and tribes; names of specific deities, religions, and members of religions; names of departments, degrees and courses; names of historical movements, periods, events, and official documents. Common nouns, which refer more generally to objects, places, or people, are not capitalized.

Proper Nouns	Common Nouns
Uncle George	my uncle
Professor Whetung	a university professor
Sioux City	the city
Ministry of Transportation	a provincial ministry
the Prime Minister	the acting prime minister
Prime Minister Pierre Trudeau	the former prime minister
New Democratic Party	a socialist party
Pollution Probe	an environmental lobby group
England, an English garden	a formal garden
Mohawk, Afro-American	a native group, white, black
God, Catholicism, Catholic	a god, a religious person
Geography Department	studying geography
Geography 101	my geography courses
Trent University	a small university
Master of Arts	a master's degree
the Enlightenment	the eighteenth century
World War II	a war
Bill 101	federal legislation

2. **Names of Languages and Derivatives**
   Any word that is also the name, or derived from the name, of a language is always capitalized.

Spanish class	math class
French Canadian	my history essay
a German major	a language major

3. **Compass Directions, Seasons, and Geographic Regions**
   These are not capitalized unless they are part of a name (e.g., North Bay) or designate a particular region of the world (e.g., the Far North) rather than a compass direction (the north of Canada).

north, the north of Canada	North Bay, the Far North
south, a southern state	the South, South Carolina

east, eastern Newfoundland	the Far East, the Eastern Townships
west, western Canadian grain	the West, the Western world
spring, summer,	the Spring Gala
fall, winter	the Winter Festival
a prairie, across the prairie	the Prairie provinces (Alberta, Saskatchewan, and Manitoba)
maritime regions	the Maritime provinces, the Maritimes (Nova Scotia, New Brunswick, and Prince Edward Island)
arctic temperatures	the Arctic; the Arctic Circle

4. **Adjectives derived from the names of legislative bodies**

Senate reform
a House committee

5. **The *plural* forms of words such as government, department, river, and state**
These are not capitalized even when they designate specific bodies.

the State Department	the departments of Finance, Transportation, and Fisheries
the Kluane River	the Kluane and Mackenzie rivers
New York State	the New England states

6. **The title of an individual**
This is capitalized only for a political or judicial office-holder, not for an officer in the private sector or in an organization or appointed government body.

| Judge Granby | council chairman David Cooke |
| Premier Harris | union president Deb Nichols |

7. **Periods of time**

These are often capitalized when the reference is to a specific historical era; otherwise they are usually in lower case. When in doubt, follow the capitalization used in the majority of your sources.

the Age of Reason	an age of reason
the Middle Ages	antiquity
the Renaissance	the renaissance of art
the Reformation	the reformation of tax laws
the Enlightenment	this enlightened era
the Dirty Thirties	the thirties
the Gay Nineties	the nineties

8. **Nouns and adjectives designating religious, philosophical, literary, artistic, and musical movements and styles**

These are capitalized when they are derivatives of proper names (e.g., Cartesian, Victorian) or when it is necessary to distinguish the name of a style or movement from the same words used in a general sense. Otherwise, lower-case letters are used.

the Group of Seven	a group of seven painters
Impressionism	such impressionism is too subjective
the Realist novel	he/she is a realist
Romanticism	a romantic movie
Sensationalism	TV serves up a lot of sensationalism
Victorian	

9. **Titles**

In the text of your essay, the first and last words of a title are always capitalized, as are all other major words of a title. Coordinating conjunctions, articles, and short prepositions are not considered major words and are not capitalized. Always capitalize a word following a colon in a title, even if it is a coordinating conjunction, article, or preposition. For titles of works in other languages, follow the conventions of the particular language.

Book Titles	Article Titles
History of Psychology	"Private Lives, Public Virtues"
A Tale of Two Cities	"How to Have an Extraordinary Life"
The World of the Short Story	
John Milton: Complete Poems and Major Prose	
The Oxford Companion to Canadian History and Literature	
Poets Between the Wars	

Some newspapers and journals do not have an article on their masthead or title page; their names, therefore, do not include an article. In these cases, if an article is needed to refer to the periodical, it should not be capitalized:

> Her book is reviewed in the *Journal of Canadian Studies*, but she subscribes only to the *American Historical Review*.

When a word in a title is hyphenated, capitalize the letter after the hyphen if the second word is of equal importance to the first (this is usually the case). If the second word only complements the first, or if the two words together are usually considered one word, do not capitalize the initial letter of the second word.

Book Titles
Problem-Solving Strategies for Writing
A History of the Re-establishment of Order

Article Titles
"Attitudes Toward Single-Parent Families"
"Neo-populism in Modern Development Theory"

For titles in reference lists, there are different styles of capitalization. In the social sciences and sciences, it is usual to capitalize only the first word, the first word after a colon or a dash, and all proper nouns in the titles of books and articles listed in the list of references. All major words in the titles of periodicals are capitalized. Look at the sample entries for the various styles to determine how to capitalize titles appearing in your list of references.

Italics

Computers make the use of italics easy. However, if you do not have a computer or printer with the capability for italics, underlining is fine in its place. The following are usually put in italics:

1. **Titles in the text**

a) Italicize the titles of published books, periodicals, microfilm publications, pamphlets, plays, films, television and radio programs, long poems that have been published as books, collections of poetry, musical compositions, dance works, paintings, and sculptures. Sacred texts or parts of sacred texts are neither italicized nor enclosed in quotation marks. If you are underlining, you may choose either to underline spaces between words in a title or not to underline them, but be consistent. Enclose in quotation marks (do not put in italics or underline) the titles of works that appear within larger works: the titles of articles and essays, chapters and sections of books (including introductions and prefaces), episodes of television and radio programs, single poems that are part of a collection of poetry, and songs or parts of longer musical compositions. Unpublished works like theses, dissertations, lectures, and speeches are usually placed in quotation marks as well.

Books
Red Earth: Revolution in a Sichuan Village
Le Rouge et le Noir

Parts of Books
"The Long Trek Home: Margaret Laurence's Stories"
  (article in *Margaret Laurence: An Appreciation*)
"The Commercial Value of Imperialism"
  (chapter in *Imperialism)*

Periodicals
Journal of Canadian Studies
Maclean's
The Globe and Mail

Articles in Periodicals
A recent *Psychology Today* article is entitled "How to Choose a President."
The *Globe and Mail* article "Mainstream AIDS Theory Challenged by Scientists" reports that the HIV virus is not the sole cause of AIDS.

Pamphlet
Towards Equity in Communication

Play
Waiting for Godot

Film
Triumph of the Will
Vertigo

Works on Television and Radio

Programs	Episodes
Star Trek	"Detective Data"
Nature	"Land of the Eagle"

Poems

Long Poems	Short poems
The Waste Land	"The Journey of the Magi"
The Faerie Queene	"The Ruines of Time"
The Odyssey	

Collections of Poetry
Songs of Innocence
Flowers for Hitler

Musical Compositions and Recordings

Musical Works	Songs or parts of longer musical works
Rigoletto	"La Donna è mobile"
The Sound of Music	"My Favorite Things"
Sgt. Pepper's Lonely Hearts Club Band	"Strawberry Fields Forever"

Note that long musical compositions that are identified by form, number, and key rather than by name are not italicized or underlined: Beethoven's Symphony no.9 in D minor or Beethoven's Ninth Symphony.

Dance Works
Swan Lake

Art Works

Paintings	Sculpture
Starry Night	*David*
Guernica	*Bird in Space*

Note that designations or names assigned to art works that are not actual titles are not italicized and are capitalized only if they are proper nouns: Mona Lisa, Venus.

Sacred works are not italicized:
The Bible
The Book of the Dead
Genesis
The Vedas
The Koran
The Dead Sea Scrolls

b) Put the title in italics as it appears on the title page. In some cases, particularly with newspapers and journals and certain classic works, the title may not include an initial definite article (the). Do not, therefore, include "the" as part of the title: write the *Iliad*, the *Divine Comedy*, the *University of Toronto Quarterly*. On the other hand, capitalize *and* italicize the initial definite article if it appears in the title: *The Globe and Mail*, *The Canadian Forum*.

c) Consult the "Documentation" section of this book to see how to capitalize and italicize titles in citations, notes, bibliographies, and lists of references. These titles are not treated the same as titles in the text.

2. **Foreign words and abbreviations**
   Italicize only those that have not been thoroughly anglicized through usage:

Weltanschauung	legerdemain	a priori
mens rea	forte	et al.
mutatis mutandis	genre	per se
caveat emptor	aide-de-camp	vis-à-vis

3. **Genera, species, and varieties**
   Do not italicize divisions larger than genus (e.g., phylum, class, order, family):

Homo sapiens	Primates
Acer saccharum	Aceraceae

4. **Quantity symbols and letters**
   Italicize those representing unknowns (e.g., X or x), but not unit symbols such as km (kilometre) or kg (kilogram).

5. **Words that the writer wants to emphasize**
   Do not italicize a word (or place it in quotation marks) simply because you feel it is not quite acceptable. If you italicize for the sake of emphasis, do so only occasionally. If you italicize a word in a quotation for emphasis, be sure to indicate that the emphasis is yours:

   > As Epictetus tells us, "If you wish to be a writer, *write*" (emphasis added).

Numbers

In arts papers, it is usual to spell out numbers that can be written in one or two words (for example, one, three hundred, nine million). Other numbers are usually given in figures:

The 138 survivors had walked over one thousand kilometres.

There are some exceptions to this rule, including numbers which express dates, numbers which express percentages, numbers used with a dollar symbol ($), and numbers with decimals:

> Company profits between April 1 and June 30, 2000 were 17 per cent higher than in the previous three months.

> The average contribution was $7.00, which is 2.5 times greater than the average in 1972.

In scientific papers, use figures to express numbers 10 and above and to express measurements. Use words to express numbers below 10 that do not represent precise measurements:

> Each day 3 g of the substance was added to the food of the 16 animals in the second group.

In essays in both the arts and the sciences, avoid beginning a sentence with a number; if you must begin with a number, spell it out. Also, if figures must be used for some numbers in a sentence or paragraph, then use figures for all numbers applicable to the same category. In other words, consistency is important.

Use the following conventions when indicating inclusive numbers: for numbers 1 to 99, write both numbers in full (e.g., 31-36); for larger numbers (including dates), write the last two digits of the second number (e.g., 105-07, 1984-85) unless more digits are needed to describe the list clearly (e.g., 96-105, 1513-654).

Expressions of Measurement

In arts papers, spell out units of measurement; do not use abbreviations even if a number is given.

> Each man's pack weighed twenty-five kilograms or more.
> (Do not write twenty-five kg.)

In scientific papers, units of measurement should be spelled out in full *unless* they are preceded by numbers:

> The distance was measured in centimetres.
> Copper wire, 18 cm long, was used to join these points.

Use only standard abbreviations. Standard abbreviations for SI units (the International System of Units) can be found in the *Metric Practice Guide*, a publication of the Canadian Standards Association.

Confusion sometimes arises between "per cent" and "percentage." The first is used *only* when a particular measurement is given. In the sciences, "per cent" may be replaced by "%."[1]

> There was an increase in volume of 112 per cent (*or* 112%).
> The percentage of people who failed was low.

Equations and Formulae
Distinguish equations and formulae from the text by isolating them on a line. Put letters used as variables or statistical symbols in italics. Identify each equation or formula with a number (usually in parentheses at the right) so that you can refer to it easily later in the paper:

> If "R" is the resistance and "d" the diameter, then

$$R = k/d^2 \qquad (1)$$

> for some constant "k."

---

[1] We have spelled "per cent" as two words following the standard British spelling. The standard American spelling is "percent."

PART III
A. DOCUMENTATION

What is Documentation?

Documentation is the systematic practice of acknowledging your sources by giving full and accurate information about the author, title, date of publication, and other related facts.

Documentation requires

- citations in the body of the essay composed of either superscript footnote/endnote numbers or parentheses containing source information;
- a final page or pages listing your sources; depending on the method used, this is titled **Bibliography, Works Cited** or **References**.

Why Document?

Documentation serves three main purposes:

1. It allows the reader of your essay to locate material you have used to check its accuracy, to read it in its original context, or to seek further information.

2. It can increase the credibility of the argument presented. When the reader can see that a fact comes from a reliable source, or that a conclusion was reached not only by the author of the paper but also by a reputable scholar in the field, the reader is more likely to be persuaded by the overall argument.

3. It is quite simply a way of acknowledging sources and avoiding plagiarism (the passing off of someone else's words or thoughts as your own).

There are different methods of documentation. You must choose a method and follow its conventions consistently throughout your essay. The method you choose depends on the discipline for which you are writing your essay. Each discipline has its preferred method of documentation. There are four principal methods:

Method One: **Footnoting/Endnoting** - used primarily in humanities disciplines such as history and classical studies

Method Two: **Parenthetical Documentation Style A** - recommended by the Modern Language Association (MLA) and used primarily in humanities disciplines such as English literature and philosophy

Method Three: **Parenthetical Documentation Style B** - recommended by the American Psychological Association (APA) and used primarily in social sciences such as psychology and political science

Method Four: **Number-Reference Method** - recommended by the Council of Biology Editors (CBE) and used primarily in natural or physical sciences such as chemistry, physics, and mathematics

Part III-C (pp. 137-62) lists the documentation methods preferred by academic disciplines and indicates some of the variations that occur within styles depending on the field of study. **When writing an essay, check this section first to determine which documentation style to follow, then turn to Part III-B, which describes each method in detail. Follow the appropriate method consistently.**

The Proper Use of Sources

Your essay belongs to you. Resist the temptation of letting the authors of your sources speak for you. Most of your essay should contain *your* discussion and analysis. However, your discussion and analysis are based on your research. Every thoroughly researched essay will make use of facts and ideas found in a number of sources. Therein lies the difficulty: sometimes every fact and idea in a research paper seems to originate in another source.

Keeping in mind the purposes of documentation makes it easier to decide what to document. The following guidelines may also help you:

Document the following:

- someone else's words;

- someone else's facts and ideas;

- someone else's organizational patterns; if you order and develop your ideas following the same pattern as your source, you must acknowledge this.

Do not document the following:

- common knowledge in the discipline; often the original source of this type of information is either unknown, widely known, or inconsequential (for example, in a Canadian politics essay, you need not document that Canadian federal politics is based on constitutional democracy);

- results of your own, original research.

Primary and Secondary Sources

It is important to be able to distinguish between these two kinds of source when researching.

Primary Sources
Primary sources are original, first-hand accounts. They might be public records, statistics, maps, manuscripts, government documents, letters, minutes, newspaper announcements, charts, or original works of literature. **A primary source is information, an artifact, or creative writing without any accompanying interpretation.** If you are writing an essay about *Great Expectations*, then the primary source is that novel, not texts of literary criticism about that novel. In the study of history, primary sources provide the raw evidence. When you consult primary sources, it is you who will analyse and interpret this evidence.

Secondary Sources

Secondary sources are most often articles, editorials, textbooks, and books that interpret other texts and works of literature, data, ideas, or events. The information they yield has been observed or gathered and interpreted by someone other than you. When your essay is centred on secondary material, it is a response to other commentators and researchers—you are entering into a dialogue with them and commenting on primary material indirectly. You must be able to assess your sources critically and use them appropriately to strengthen the points you are making.

Summarizing and Paraphrasing

Summarizing means stating, in your own words, a source's main ideas or points. A summary does not include the source's supporting details or evidence and is therefore shorter and more concise than its source. Paraphrasing means giving, in your own words, a precise re-statement of your source's facts and ideas. Paraphrasing does not necessarily mean shortening, and it usually follows the structure and organizational pattern of the source.

When to Summarize

Summarize when your reader needs to know only the main points of the source you are consulting and doesn't need to know your source's supporting details and evidence, or *how* the points are made. Often the requirements of your essay dictate that only the main (or selected) points of a source are necessary to support your discussion. Even if you have taken detailed notes, summarize them if that is the most effective way to use them. Be aware, however, that too much summarizing will make your essay too general. Summary should be complemented with quotations and some important details.

When to Paraphrase

Paraphrase passages or sections of a source when your essay requires detailed information or ideas from that section. It is not practical to paraphrase a chapter or much more than one page. Paraphrasing works best for two to three paragraphs; anything longer you should probably summarize.

Summarizing and paraphrasing are effective ways of presenting what you have learned from your research. Both allow you to come to a better understanding of what you have read because you must try to say it yourself. Both force you to read closely and accurately and to find the meaning in often complex texts.

Remember, if you do not use your own words, you are quoting, not summarizing or paraphrasing, and quoting requires the use of quotation marks. Otherwise, you will be plagiarizing. To avoid this, take notes from your sources in point form and then restate the information using sentences and words that come naturally to you. Don't feel you have to use synonyms for your source's words, but do so if a synonym is more natural or likely for you. Don't think that reproducing a source's sentence structure with a few nouns and verbs changed to synonyms constitutes either paraphrase or summary. Use your own sentence structure; otherwise, you are using a source's organizational pattern (a sentence is an organizational pattern), and that requires documentation.

Skilful paraphrasing and summarizing are acquired techniques.

Remember to

- use your own words, phrasing, and sentence structure
- read over your sentences to make sure they are your own and that they make sense

For more on avoiding plagiarism, see pp. 44-47.

Quotations

You can support your ideas and make your essay lively and interesting with well-chosen quotations. Because quotations are first-hand evidence of the contributors to your thought, quoting your sources is desirable, even expected. This is particularly so when writing a humanities paper. Rather than detracting from your work, well-chosen quotations add to it, giving your argument validity and support. You should be careful, however, to use quotations sparingly, because using them to support your ideas is one thing, allowing them to take control of your paper is quite another. However, carefully selected quotations provide useful contextual information and supportive data, and they complement accurate paraphrase and succinct summary.

If your quotations are to be effective, they must be an integral part of your essay. Resist the temptation to throw in a quotation merely because it sounds impressive and has, you feel, *something* to do with your subject. Have a reason for using a quotation. The following guidelines will help you.

When to Quote

- when the writer's style or eloquence is so memorable that summarizing or paraphrasing would be significantly less effective
- when the writer's words give your argument validity and support
- when you want to comment on, agree with, disagree with or otherwise take exception to, what the writer has said
- when you want to comment specifically on the writer's use of words

How to Quote

Make sure to introduce the quotation so that it is linked clearly and smoothly with your thoughts. After the quotation, make sure that you supply any needed explanations of or comments on the quotation. Do not assume that your reader will interpret the quotation exactly as you have.

Attribution

To attribute, when you are writing an essay, means to explicitly acknowledge and name the source of your quotation in the text of your essay.

> *Example*:
> McKenzie reports, "The reproductive capacity of the blue whale was the lowest of all baleen species."

Why attribute?

Why not? It is not necessary to create the illusion that your essay has not benefited from others' ideas. Sometimes the easiest, clearest way to present your material is by attributing. In addition, readers often need to know the author and other circumstances in order to interpret and evaluate a quotation accurately. A serious problem would arise if a student were to write,

> The claim has been made that "if one consults only absolute figures, unmarried persons seem to commit suicide less than married ones" (Durkheim, 1951:171).

As is, this sentence and citation lead the reader to believe that Durkheim made the claim. However, if the reader were to look at the source, it would be clear that the writer may have found the quotation in a book by Durkheim, but somebody else actually made the claim. An accurate citation with correct attribution would read,

> In 1897, Emile Durkheim used systematic statistical investigation to disprove the claim of Bertillon Sr. that "if one consults only absolute figures, unmarried persons seem to commit suicide less than married ones" (Durkheim, 1951:171).

The claim is now attributed to its correct author by naming him in the text.

The remainder of this section is divided into three main parts:

1. Quoting accurately
2. Quoting prose
3. Quoting poetry

In each section, examples are given of well-integrated, correctly punctuated quotations. Use these as guides for your own quotations.

Quoting Accurately
Always indicate a quotation by using quotation marks to open and close the borrowed passage or (for longer extracts as described below) by indenting. Ensure that the quotation corresponds exactly with the wording, spelling, and punctuation of the original; any changes that you make in the quotation must be indicated by using ellipsis dots (three spaced periods) or square brackets.

Ellipsis

Use ellipsis dots wherever you omit material from what you are quoting. Type three periods, spacing before and after each one, to indicate an omission within a sentence. If an omission occurs between two sentences, type four periods. It is not necessary, however, to use ellipsis dots at the beginning of a quoted passage. Newer practice for humanities essays (based on MLA style) is to place square brackets around the ellipsis dots [. . .]. Leave a space after the first and second dots, but not after the final dot within the bracket. Leave a space before the opening bracket and after the closing bracket. If the ellipsis ends the sentence, a period is still needed outside the bracket to end the sentence. Note the placement and spacing of the ellipsis dots in the following examples.

Examples:

omission of part of a sentence:

"Previous fossil discoveries there . . . include trilobites of middle Cambrian age."

"Previous fossil discoveries there [. . .] include trilobites of middle Cambrian age."

omission of a complete sentence:

"Bedford was well known and appreciated for his ability to engage his audiences. . . . Michael Sidnell's review of *The School for Wives* describes the energy and dramatic flair that Bedford brought to the role of Arnolphe and won for him the full acclaim — even the love — of his audience."

"Bedford was well known and appreciated for his ability to engage his audiences. [. . .] Michael Sidnell's review of *The School for Wives* describes the energy and dramatic flair that Bedford brought to the role of Arnolphe and won for him the full acclaim — even the love — of his audience."

omission from the middle of a sentence to the end of that sentence or another sentence:

"He didn't just play to the gallery, he found somebody up there
to point to . . . . His audience would gladly have given this
Arnolphe the girl, the money and, of course, the palm."

"He didn't just play to the gallery, he found somebody up there
to point to [. . .]. His audience would gladly have given this
Arnolphe the girl, the money and, of course, the palm."

Square brackets
Use square brackets if you wish to insert in the quotation a word or
more of explanation.

> *Example*:
> "The task [of the commission] is to investigate the alleged illegal
> activities of the RCMP."

Because a quotation should fit into your sentence or paragraph as an
integral part of your language and meaning, it is sometimes necessary
to change a capital letter (e.g., one beginning a sentence in the quoted
source) to a lower-case letter. Square brackets are used to make this
change also.

> *Example*:
> Robert Seton-Watson stressed that "[i]n our Victorian dislike of
> the practice of calling a spade a bloody shovel, it is not necessary
> to go to the opposite extreme of calling it an agricultural
> implement."

"Sic"
If you wish to indicate that your quotation is accurate even though the
passage's spelling, language or logic is faulty, place the word *sic*
within square brackets following the error.

> *Example*:
> These children "gave evidence that there [*sic*] ability to put
> events in sequence was severely impaired."

Quoting Prose

a. **Short Quotations**

Prose quotations of four typed lines or fewer are usually incorporated into the text of the essay and are enclosed within quotation marks.

b. **Long quotations**

Use longer quotations sparingly. You can often make your point better with a short selection than with a longer one. However, long quotations are sometimes necessary to preserve accuracy and completeness of meaning. Indent every line of a long quotation and double-space throughout. **Quotation marks are not used unless they appear within the text of the quoted material.**

c. **Punctuation to Introduce Quotations**

1. If you work the quotation into the structure of your sentence, **no introductory or additional punctuation is necessary**.

   Example:
   The bodies of the natives were not painted in brilliant colours but rather "in the subdued colours provided by earth and rock."

2. If you use **attributory words**, i.e., words that identify the speaker or the writer of the passage and an explicit verb of saying (or stating, writing, observing, noting etc.), use **commas** to set off these words, whether they appear before, after, or between parts of the quotation.

   Examples:

   attributory words before:

   McKenzie reports, "The reproductive capacity of the blue whale was the lowest of all baleen species."

   attributory words between:

   "The reproductive capacity of the blue whale," McKenzie reports, "was the lowest of all baleen species."

attributory words at the end:

"The reproductive capacity of the blue whale was the lowest of all baleen species," McKenzie reports.

3. If you precede your quotation with **an independent clause**, use a **colon** to introduce the quotation. The independent clause, which could be punctuated as a sentence in its own right, introduces the idea or the context of the quotation which follows.

    Examples:
    Hedley Bull is quite clear on this point: "We are accustomed, in the modern world, to contrast war between states with peace between states; but the historical alternative to war between states was more ubiquitous violence."

    Rea and McLeod outline the three fundamental concepts of socialism:

    > First, socialists have desired to substitute public ownership for private ownership of the principal means of production. Second, socialists have emphasizeed equality of opportunity, which, they maintain, is neither present nor possible under capitalism. Third, since the 1930s, socialists have emphasized the concept of "economic planning" and have wished to substitute planning for the so-called "automatic," or "self-regulating," market.

d. Punctuation to Close Short Quotations

1. Periods or commas at the close of a quotation are placed before the quotation marks unless parenthetical material follows the quotation, in which case the comma or period is placed after the closing parenthesis.

    Examples:
    Ultimately, we see King Lear as a victim, "a man more sinned against than sinning."

Michael Sidnell writes that Bedford "didn't just play to the gallery, he found somebody up there to point to, and another collaborative spectator in the stalls below" (153).

2. Punctuation marks other than periods or commas are placed outside the quotation marks except when they are part of quoted material. Parenthetical citations are still placed directly before the end punctuation.

Examples:
What does Hunter mean by "haphazard urban agglomeration" (145)?

Wood begins by asking, "What is an ethnic group?" (64).

e. **Punctuation to Close Long Quotations**

Parenthetical citations are placed *after* end punctuation in long, indented quotations:

Example:
Cook and Newson discuss Chomsky's argument:

> The argument partly depends on two requirements
> which, though Chomsky does not name them
> explicitly himself, can be called occurrence and
> uniformity. It is not enough to show that some
> aspects of the environment logically could help the
> child; we must show that it *does* occur. While it is at
> least conceivable that parental explanation of the
> Binding Principles might be highly useful to the
> child, it is inconceivable that it actually occurs. If a
> model of acquisition depends crucially on children
> hearing a particular structure or on their being
> corrected by their parents, it is necessary to show
> that this actually happens; to meet the occurrence
> requirement, speculations about the evidence that
> children might encounter need support from

observations of what they *do* encounter. (1996, p. 91; emphasis in original)

f. Punctuating Quotations within Quotations

Use single quotation marks if you have already used double marks around the entire passage. IN other words, when quoting a sentence that contains quotation marks already, place double marks around all the words you are quoting and turn the double quotation marks of the original into single marks.

Example:
From then on "Balfour was no longer Knox's 'faithful brother,' but 'blasphemous Balfour,' the 'principal misguider now of Scotland,' who above all others ought to be abhorred."

Quoting Poetry

Quoting poetry is not much different from quoting prose, so follow the guidelines above in "Quoting Prose," keeping the following in mind.

a. Short Quotations
It is best to incorporate verse quotations of a single line or shorter into the structure of your sentence.

Example:
Coleridge's ancient Mariner is described as having a "long grey beard and glittering eye" (3).

Selections of two lines may be incorporated in the same way, but with the lines separated by a slash (/). Include a space before and after each slash.

Example:
An example of alliteration occurs in the lines "And jealous of the listening air / They steal their way from stair to stair" (167-68).

44

b. Long Quotations

Longer quotations should be indented ten spaces from the left margin and set line for line as they are printed in the original. Don't use quotation marks unless they appear in the original text of the poem.

> *Example*:
>> The hand which still held Juan's, by degrees
>> Gently, but palpably confirmed its grasp,
>> As if it said, "Detain me, if you please";
>> Yet there's no doubt she only meant to clasp
>> His fingers with a pure Platonic squeeze. (I.111)

If you omit a line, or several lines or stanzas, indicate this by a line of ellipsis dots.

> *Example*:
>> It is an ancient Mariner,
>> And he stoppeth one of three.
>> "By thy long grey beard and glittering eye,
>> Now wherefore stopp'st thou me? ["]
>> ....
>> He holds him with his glittering eye —
>> The Wedding-Guest stood still,
>> And listens like a three years' child:
>> The Mariner hath his will. (1-16)

Avoiding Plagiarism

Plagiarism — passing off someone else's words or thoughts as your own — is a serious academic offence. The student who plagiarizes may expect to receive at least a reprimand and possibly a failure in the essay or course, depending upon the circumstances and the kind of plagiarism involved.

The worst kind of plagiarism, of course, is submitting an essay written in whole or in part by someone else. Even copying a short passage constitutes plagiarism unless the student encloses the passage in quotation marks and acknowledges the source. But the student who changes only the odd word in someone else's sentences is also (perhaps unwittingly) committing plagiarism, as is one who relies heavily on secondary sources for the argument, organization, and main points of his or her paper. Even the properly documented paraphrasing of someone else's writing constitutes plagiarism if the paraphrase contains phrasing from the original that is not enclosed in quotation marks.

Remember, as well, that you should not copy lines or paragraphs verbatim from essays that you have previously submitted and for which you have received a grade. Even though the ideas expressed in these lines belong to you, you are not free to quote sections of your old essays without any documentation. Because your ideas will continue to develop throughout your university career, it is understandable that some of your themes and concepts are likely to resurface in papers dealing with the same or similar subjects. Nevertheless, the expression of these thoughts and ideas should always be revised to fit every new context.

Plagiarism occurs when facts or ideas not commonly known or held in the field are presented in an essay without the required documentation. **When in the least doubt, document the source.** You can avoid committing plagiarism unwittingly by reading widely in the discipline and by using good research and notetaking techniques. See "Researching the Essay" (p. 7) and the "The Proper Use of Sources" (p. 28).

Examine the following illustrations carefully.

Illustration 1

Suppose you wanted to quote from the following passage from *Modern England* by R.K. Webb:

> **By the middle of Victoria's reign,** therefore, the Established Church **was dominated by two groups** who earlier in the century had been **minorities** — the Tractarians and their Anglo-Catholic heirs, the Evangelicals. Both the Tractarians and the Evangelicals **agreed that the enemy was religious liberalism,** but beyond that, there was no possibility of accommodation between them.

This is what appears in your essay (the bolded words in both passages indicate where the wording is identical):

The Established Church was undergoing a marked change
by the middle of Victoria's reign. It was dominated by
two groups, the Tractarians and the Evangelicals, and both
of these former religious minorities agreed that the enemy
was religious liberalism.

If you were to write this you would be guilty of plagiarism because not
only is the source of the information undocumented but, and just as
important, the passage follows the wording of the original very
closely.

The right thing to do would be to quote this information and
document it appropriately:

R.K. Webb points out that "[b]y the middle of Victoria's
reign . . . the Established Church was dominated by two
groups who earlier in the century had been minorities — the
Tractarians and their Anglo-Catholic heirs, the Evangelicals.
Both . . . agreed that the enemy was religious liberalism."

Illustration 2

The following excerpt is contained in an entry on Sigmund Freud in the
third edition of *Benet's Reader's Encyclopedia*:

Freud postulated the existence of three internal forces
that govern a person's psychic life: (1) the *id*, the
instinctual force of life — unconscious, uncontrollable, and
isolated; (2) the *ego*, the executive force that has contact
with the real world; (3) the *super-ego*, the governing force,
or moral conscience, that seeks to control and direct the ego
into socially acceptable patterns of behavior.

An inexperienced writer, incorrectly assuming that essays are simply a
compilation of facts gleaned from various sources, might write the
following without documentation:

Freud claimed that people had three internal forces that
governed their psychic life: the *id*, which is instinctual; the

ego, which is the executive force based on reality; and the *super-ego,* which is the governing force directing the ego into acceptable patterns of behaviour.

Again, as well as being undocumented, the passage contains too many sequences and syntactical patterns borrowed directly from the original without enough paraphrase or interpretation. Note, however, that if the student wrote the following, it would not be considered an act of plagiarism because Freud's concepts are now considered common knowledge, and this information can be found in many different sources. Using the words "psychic," "id," "ego," and "super-ego" is, in this instance, not plagiarism:

The three psychic forces first described by Sigmund Freud were the *id,* the *ego,* and the *super-ego.*

In addition, the writer has paraphrased the source and presented the main ideas using his or her own syntactical pattern.

PART III
B. METHODS OF DOCUMENTATION

This section describes in detail each of the methods of documentation. Decide which one you wish to follow by referring to the following section on preferred documentation style by academic discipline. Each section shows you how to cite your sources in the text of your essay and how to properly list your sources on a page attached to your essay.

Method One: Footnoting/Endnoting

For many years, the footnoting/endnoting method was standard for documenting sources, and some schools, disciplines, and scholarly journals in the humanities continue to recommend it. It is the preferred method when authors and readers want full references to relate closely to the text and therefore has important scholarly implications in disciplines such as **history, classical literature, and philosophy**.

How to Footnote/ Endnote
(Use *either* footnoting *or* endnoting in your essay.)

Superscript Numbering
Text to be documented is indicated by small Arabic superscript numbers (e.g., [1,2,3]). The footnote for each appears at the bottom of the page on which the superscript citation appears. Endnotes are listed at the end of the essay on separate pages which immediately precede the bibliography.

In the text of the essay, the superscript numbers are placed after the end punctuation of the sentence in which the cited material is incorporated.

Example:
As Bismarck once remarked, the next great war in Europe would be set off by "some damned foolish thing in the Balkans."[1]

or

"Some damned foolish thing in the Balkans," Bismarck once remarked, would set off the next great European war.[1]

However, if there is any possibility that paraphrased or quoted material might be confused with your original material, place the number **within** the sentence and immediately following the material from another source; or, in the case of quoted material, place the number immediately following the closing quotation mark.

Example:
"Some damned foolish thing in the Balkans,"[1] Bismarck once remarked, would set off the next great European war, and that thing was Serb nationalism, which was embodied in two famous political organizations: *Narodna Odbrana* and *Ujedinjenje ili Smrt.*[2]

The superscript number should follow all punctuation marks except the dash.

The Footnote/Endnote

The footnote/endnote gives all the publishing information and the page reference necessary to indicate the specific location of the item borrowed from or referred to. The footnote/endnote begins with the same superscript number as the one which appears in the text at the end of the material the footnote/endnote will document. Footnotes/endnotes are numbered consecutively and the numbering is carried on throughout the essay.

- **Footnotes** appear at the bottom of the page. Many computer programs will position and number footnotes automatically.
- **Endnotes** are listed on pages following the text of the essay. These pages are numbered in sequence with the rest of the essay. On the first page, the title "Notes" is centred and placed one inch from the top of the page. Leave two blank lines before entering the first note.
- In the examples in this book, single spacing is used in footnotes and endnotes, but you should double space within and between footnotes and endnotes.

- The first footnote^{**} to a source is the only one that gives full publishing information. Note that the format is like a paragraph, the first line being indented.

Example:
    ¹Fred Flintstone, Barney Rubble, and Betty Rubble, "Ode to Wilma," *The Collected Works of Fred Flintstone: A Tribute to Neolithic Creativity*, ed. Arnold A. Anthropologist, 2nd ed., vol. 4 of 5 vols., Prehistoric Verse 17 (New York: Cambrian P, 2000) 18. In 2100, Cambrian plans to publish a commemorative edition that will include an introduction by Bam Bam.

In **second and subsequent footnotes** to a source, use a shortened form of the first note. Give only enough information to identify the work; the author's last name and the page numbers are usually enough.

Example:
    ²Brody 19.

If two or more works by the same author are referred to in the essay, you should give a shortened form of the title after the author's name:

Example:
    ³Gibbon, *Decline and Fall* 160. (instead of *The History of the Decline and Fall of the Roman Empire*)

    ⁴Gibbon, *Memoirs* 25. (instead of *Memoirs of my Life*)

The Latin abbreviations "Ibid.," "Op. Cit.," and "Loc. Cit." are no longer used, so follow the preceding instructions, even if two identical footnotes occur in sequence.

Variations on the Standard Footnote
Citing One Source Frequently
When you are citing one source frequently in your essay, second and subsequent references to the source may be made in the body of the essay simply by giving the relevant page numbers (or act, scene, and

---

^{**}Throughout the rest of this section, "footnote" is used to describe both footnotes and endnotes.

line numbers) in parentheses. In your first footnote reference to the source, indicate that you plan to cite subsequent references to that source in the text of the essay.

Example:
[5]Charles Dickens, *The Personal History of David Copperfield*, ed. Trevor Blount (Harmondsworth, England: Penguin, 1966) 154. Subsequent references to this work will be from this edition and will be parenthetically cited by page number in the text.

Several major sources of a paper can be documented in this way. To keep the sources straight, the parenthetical reference will contain a surname, an abbreviated title if needed for clarity, and the appropriate page numbers.

Citing an Indirect Source
Sometimes you may wish to quote or refer to the work of an author as you found it in the work of another author. Cite both, writing "qtd. in" before giving the reference for the source in which you found the material.

Example:
You might write,

As J.B. Priestley writes, "I had no direct evidence but I soon came to believe—and friends more in the know than I was agreed with me—that it was Churchill who had me taken off the air."[6]

However, as you did not find this quotation in a book by Priestley, but in one by Joseph Lash, your footnote would look like this:

[6]J.B. Priestley, *All England Listened* (New York, 1967) xx, qtd. in Joseph P. Lash, *Roosevelt and Churchill, 1939-1941: The Partnership That Saved the West* (New York: Norton, 1976) 278.

If the publication information is not available for the original source, give the author's name only, followed by "qtd. in."

Supplementary Footnotes

Footnotes, besides giving documentation, may also provide information which cannot be easily incorporated into your text. Supplementary footnotes usually define, amplify, or qualify material you are discussing, or they refer the reader to other sources. They can be used with both the parenthetical and footnoting methods of documentation:

Example:
    [7]These conclusions have also been reached by L. Baird, "Big School, Small School: A Critical Examination of the Hypothesis," *Journal of Educational Psychology* 60 (1969): 253-60.

The First Footnote to a Source: Examples

Here are examples of what first footnotes look like depending on the kind of source you are using. Some of your citations will not conform exactly to any of the examples given. In this case, **find and follow the example which most closely conforms to the source you are dealing with, adding in the necessary information as shown in other relevant examples.** The examples are divided into the following sections:

- print sources (books, articles, government documents, pamphlets, and archival material, for example);
- non-print material (including lectures, personal communication, and films); and
- electronic sources.

Documenting Print Sources
Books

Order of information:

1. Author's name, in normal order as it appears on the title page
2. Title of the part of the book used (e.g., poem, article)
3. Title of the book, as it appears on the title page
4. Name of the editor or translator
5. Edition, if other than first

6. Volume number(s)
7. Series name
8. Place of publication
9. Publisher's name
10. Date of publication
11. Page number(s)
12. Supplementary bibliographical material or comments, in complete sentences (optional)

a) **A book with a single author**

   [1]Kathryn Chittick, *Dickens and the 1830s* (Cambridge: Cambridge UP, 1990) 68.

b) **A book with a single author and an editor or translator, when references are to the author, not the editor or translator**

   [2]Charles Dickens, *The Personal History of David Copperfield*, ed. Trevor Blount (Harmondsworth, England: Penguin, 1966) 154-56.

   [3]Menander, *Plays and Fragments*, trans. Norma Miller (London: Penguin, 1987) 19-50.

c) **A book with an editor or translator, when references are to the edited material: the introduction, notes, editorial decisions regarding layout, etc.**

   [4]Trevor Blount, ed., *The Personal History of David Copperfield*, by Charles Dickens (Harmondsworth, England: Penguin, 1966) 55.

   [5]Norma Miller, trans., *Plays and Fragments*, by Menander (London: Penguin, 1987) 21.

d) A book with two or more authors
If the book has two or three authors, list all authors; if the book has four or more authors, list only the first author followed by "et al." (meaning "and oothers").

    [6]Patrick Malcolmson and Richard Myers, *The Canadian Regime* (Peterborough, ON: Broadview P, 1996) 30.

    [7]Joan Fleet, Fiona Goodchild, and Richard Zajchowski, *Learning for Success: Skills and Strategies for Canadian Students* (Toronto: Harcourt Brace, 1994) 29-31.

    [8]Mary Field Belenky, et al., *Women's Ways of Knowing: The Development of Self, Voice, and Mind* (New York: Basic, 1986) 96.

e) A book with a corporate author

    [9]Canadian Historical Association, *Regionalism in the Canadian Community 1867-1967*, ed. Mason Wade (Toronto: U of Toronto P), 1969.

f) A book with no author given
Do not use Anonymous or Anon. Begin the note with the title (ignoring articles a, an, and the).

    [10]*1990 Stoddart Restaurant Guide to Toronto* (Toronto: Stoddart, 1990) 3.

g) An edition other than the first
An edition is noted by number (e.g., 2nd ed., 3rd ed.), by year (e.g., 1990 ed.), or by name (e.g., Centennial edition, rev. ed.) in keeping with the format of the title page.

    [11]Lucille Strath, Heather Avery, and Karen Taylor, *Notes on the Preparation of Essays in the Arts and Sciences*, 4th ed. (Peterborough, ON: Academic Skills Centre, Trent U, 1993) 100.

h) **A work in several volumes**

Citation format varies depending on the actual reference. If all the volumes to which you are referring have the same title, the number of volumes is placed immediately before the publishing information.

[12]Max Weber, *Economy and Society: An Outline of Interpretive Sociology*, ed. Guenther Roth and Claus Wittich, trans. Ephraim Fischoff, et al. 3 vols. (New York: Bedminster, 1968) 1: 215-16.

If the volume you have used has a title that is different from the title of the entire collection, give the title of the single volume first. Then, after citing publication details, indicate which volume you have used, followed by the multivolume title.

[13]Irvin Ehrenpreis, *Dean Swift* (Cambridge, MA: Harvard UP, 1983) 627-31, vol. 3 of *Swift: The Man, His Works, and the Age* (Cambridge, MA: Harvard UP, 1969-83).

i) **A book in a series**

[14]Louis H. Pratt, *Alice Malsenior Walker: an Annotated Bibliography, 1968-1986*, Meckler's Studies and Bibliographies on Black Americans 1 (Westport, CT: Meckler, 1988) 54.

j) **A book with a publisher's imprint**

Publishers sometimes group some of their publications under special names, called imprints. The name of the publisher's imprint can be found on the title page usually above the publisher's name. In a footnote, the imprint (in this case, Borzoi) is given before the name of the publisher, and both names are joined with a hyphen.

[15]Bruno Bettelheim, *The Uses of Enchantment: The Meaning and Importance of Fairy Tales* (New York: Borzoi-Knopf, 1976) 235.

k) **A republished book**

When a book has been republished, give the date of the original publication inside the opening parenthesis followed by a semi-colon and the publication information.

   ¹⁶Catharine Parr Traill, *The Backwoods of Canada*, ed.
Michael Peterman, Centre for Editing Early Canadian Texts 11
(1846; Ottawa: Carleton UP, 1997) 44.

l) **A play that has act, scene, and line numbers**

Act, scene, and line numbers are separated by periods, not commas, and there is no need to give a page reference. If the author is widely known, as in the case of William Shakespeare, the author's name may be omitted. Because act, scene, and line numbers are the same in all editions of classic plays, even the edition and publication data may be omitted if this information is irrelevant to the writer's purpose.

   ¹⁷*Hamlet*, ed. Edward Hubler (New York: Signet-NAL,
1963) 3.2.73-75.

   or
      ¹⁸*Hamlet* 3.2.73-75.

Note the absence of a comma after the title in the second example.

It is preferable to use parenthetical citation in the text for references to lines of poetry or sections of plays.

Sections of Books

a) **One part of a book by a single author (e.g., poem, short story, essay, article, or chapter)**

   ¹⁹Forrest E. LaViolette, "The Potlatch Law: Wardship and Enforcement," *The Struggle for Survival: Indian Cultures and the Protestant Ethic in British Columbia* (Toronto: U of Toronto P, 1973) 90.

b) **An article in a book in which there are articles by a number of writers**

    [20]Kathleen Weiler, "You've Got to Stay There and Fight: Sex Equity, Schooling, and Work," *Changing Education: Women as Radicals and Conservators*, ed. Joyce Antler and Sari Knopp Bilen (Albany, NY: SUNY P, 1990) 220.

c) **A work in an anthology**
    If the work is a short poem, short story, or essay (in other words, a work that has probably not been previously published on its own), enclose the title of this work in quotation marks.

    [21]W. B. Yeats, "The Second Coming," *The Norton Anthology of English Literature*, ed. M.H. Abrams, 5th ed., vol. 2 (New York: Norton, 1986) 1948, lines 22-23.

If the work is a play, novel, or long poem (in other words, a work that has probably been previously published on its own), italicize the title of this work. In the example below, the reference is to the entire play, which can be found on pages 1-73. If lines of the play were being referenced, *either* the act, scene, and line *or* the page on which the lines appeared (whichever is more appropriate) would be noted.

    [22]Bernard Shaw, *Major Barbara*, *Bernard Shaw's Plays*, ed. Warren Sylvester Smith (New York: Norton, 1970) 1-73.

If your reference is to the collection as a whole, cite it as an edited text.

    [23]William Shakespeare, *William Shakespeare: The Complete Works*, ed. Alfred Harbage (Baltimore: Penguin, 1969).

d) **An introduction, preface, foreword, or afterword**
The appropriate label (e.g., Foreword) is given. If the writer of the part being cited differs from the author of the entire work, the word "by" and the author's name follow the title of the work.

[24]Herbert Lindenberger, Foreword, *MLA Style Manual and Guide to Scholarly Publishing*, by Joseph Gibaldi, 2nd ed. (New York: MLA, 1998) xvii.

e) **An article in a reference book (encyclopaedia, dictionary)**
If the article has an author, begin with that author's name in normal order. (Remember that in reference books, authorship is often indicated only by initials, usually given at the close of an article. If the author's name is abbreviated to initials, find the key to abbreviations or the list of contributing authors, and give the author's full name in your citation.)

[25]Julia Cairns, "Spry, Constance," *Dictionary of National Biography 1951-1960*, 1971 ed., 915.

If there is no author indicated, begin with the title of the article. Only the year of publication need be given for well-known multivolume reference books.

[25]"Axminster Carpets," *Encyclopaedia Britannica: Micropaedia*, 1974.

Articles in Periodicals (journals, magazines, newspapers)

Order of Information:

1. Author's name, in normal order (first name first)
2. Title of the article
3. Name of the periodical

4. Publication data: Series number or name
Volume number, in Arabic numerals
Issue number
Publication date
5. Page number(s)

Where no specific example is given (e.g., for notes on works by multiple authors), follow the general guidelines given for books.

a) **Journal articles**

An article published in a journal with continuous pagination throughout the annual volume
The volume number (83), but not the issue number, is given.

[1]David E. Bynum, "Themes of the Young Hero in Serbocroatian Oral Epic Tradition," *PMLA* 83 (1968): 1296.

An article from a journal that paginates each issue separately
The volume number (19) and the issue number (4) are both given.

[2]Edgar J. Dosman, "Hemispheric Relations in the 1980s: A Perspective from Canada," *Journal of Canadian Studies* 19.4 (1984): 55.

b) **A magazine article**
If the magazine is published monthly, the month may be listed without the day. The names of all months are abbreviated with the exceptions of May, June, and July.

[3]Robert Fulford, "Regarding Alex Colville," *Saturday Night* 17 June 2000: 34.

c) **A newspaper article**
Give the name of the newspaper without the word "the," e.g., *Globe and Mail*, not *The Globe and Mail*. When the place of publication is not part of the newspaper's title, it is added in square brackets after the title. When the newspaper has different editions,

the name of the edition that appears on the masthead is placed after the date and preceded by a comma.

[4]Shawn McCarthy, "Clock now ticking on free-trade deal," *Globe and Mail* [Toronto] 23 Apr. 2001, metro ed.: A1.

If the name of the author is not given, begin with the title of the article.

[5]"Wal-Mart heir ousts Gates as world's richest man," *National Post* [Toronto] 23 Apr. 2001: A2.

d) An editorial or a letter to an editor

[6]"Making it a Summit for all the Americas," editorial, *Globe and Mail* [Toronto] 23 Apr. 2001: A18.

[7]Theresa Manchester, letter, *National Post* [Toronto] 23 Apr. 2001: A15.

[8]Aaron Edison, letter, *Atlantic* Feb. 2000: 69.

e) A review (of a book, movie, or live performance)
The phrase "rev. of" is used to introduce the material being reviewed.

[9]Robert Cottrell, "Founding Father," rev. of *My Six Years with Gorbachev* by Anatoly S. Chernyaev, *The New York Review of Books* 26 Apr. 2001: 20-22.

For a performance review, add the relevant information, such as place of performance and name of performing company:

[10]Nancy Franklin, "Blarney Stones," rev. of *Stones in his Pockets* by Marie Jones, Golden Theatre, New York, *The New Yorker* 16 Apr. 2001: 88-89.

If the review has no title, place "rev. of" immediately after the name of the reviewer:

[11]Jenefer Phelp, rev. of *Input, Interaction and the Second Language Learner* by Susan M. Gass, *Language Awareness* 9 (2000): 115-17.

Other Sources

a) **A government document**
    When no author is given, the government body is treated as the author. The name of the government author is followed by the title of the document, italicized. When title pages are given in more than one language, only one version need be used. After the title, the available relevant publication information is given (publisher, place and date of publication, pages, etc.). Citing government documents can be complicated, but the government documents librarian or another member of the library staff will be able to help you.

    [1]Ontario Legislative Assembly, Standing Committee on Social Development, *Report on Food Banks*, 2nd session, 34th Parliament (Toronto: Government of Ontario, May 1983) S-6.

b) **A dissertation or thesis**

    Unpublished

    [2]Christine Niero, "Making Stories: Studies in Contemporary Canadian Metafiction," diss., Queen's U, 1987, 2.

    Published

    [3]A.G. Finley, *Shipbuilding in St. Martins 1840-1880: A Case Study of Family Enterprise on the Fundy Shore*, M.A. thesis, U of New Brunswick, 1980 (Ottawa: Canadian Theses on Microfiche, 1984) 47732, 18.

c) **A pamphlet**
Treat a pamphlet as you would a book. Often, publication details will be sketchy: use n.p. for "no known publisher" or "no known place of publication," n. pag. for "no pagination," and n.d. for "no date given" to indicate missing data.

    [4]*Human Rights: What to Do about Discrimination or Harassment* (Peterborough, ON: Trent U, n.d.) n. pag.

d) **Archival material**
The format for citing archival material varies; however, certain pieces of standard information are necessary in all archival citations. The citation must first enable the reader to locate the archival material by identifying the repository and the material's location within the repository; it must also describe the material as any citation would, giving author, date, etc. The National Archives of Canada is abbreviated NAC. RG stands for Record Group (the collection in the NAC where the material may be found). The material cited here can be located on pages 131 and 132 of volume 1846.

    [5]NAC RG10, vol. 1846, 131, 132, "Treaty No. 3 between Her Majesty the Queen and the Saulteaux Tribe of the Ojibbeway Indians at the Northwest Angle of the Lake of the Woods with Adhesions, 3 October 1873."

e) **A legal document/court case**
In general, a citation of a legal document must include the following: identification of case or document, date of document, and information making clear where the document can be found (name, volume, and page of court report, for example). The example below refers to a case brought before the Supreme Court of Canada.

    [6]*Law Society of British Columbia v. Andrews*, 1989, 1 S.C.R. 143.

64

f) **Material from an information service**
Cite the material from the service much the same way you would
cite other printed material, giving publication information. Add the
name of the service and the file number at the end of the entry.

[7]Liddy Limbrick, et al., *Peer-Power: Using Peer Tutoring to
Help Low-Progress Readers in Primary and Secondary Schools*
(Wellington: New Zealand Council for Educational Research,
1985) 10 (ERIC ED 326 858).

If the material has not been published previously, cite the service
as the publisher. No place of publication is needed. Retain the file
number at the end of the citation.

[8]Susan B. Thomas, "Concerns about Gifted Children: A
Paper and Abstract Bibliography" (ERIC: 1974) 23 (ERIC ED
091 083).

g) **An advertisement**

[9]Nissan, "Introducing the new Infiniti QX4,"
Advertisement, *The New Yorker* 24 Apr. 2000: 2-5.

Documenting Non-Print Sources

a) **A lecture, address, debate**
If the title of the presentation is not known, use an accurate
descriptive word (e.g., Lecture, Address, Debate). Do not italicize
this word or place it in quotation marks.

[1]John Syrett, "Nixon the Great Before Watergate," Hist.
312, Trent U, 7 Mar. 2000.

[2]James Neufeld, Zailig Pollock, and Suzanne Bailey, Debate,
Engl. 205, Trent U, 26 Mar. 2001.

b) **A personal communication (interview, letter)**
    Give the name of the person contacted, the appropriate descriptive
    label (e.g., Personal Interview, Telephone Interview, Personal
    Letter), and the date.

    [3]Judith A. O'Donoghue, Personal Interview, 9 Apr. 2001.

    For e-mail communications, follow this format:

    [4]Nadine May, "Re: Conference Paper," e-mail to the author,
    11 May 2001.

    [5]Mike Walker, "Learning Disabilities: Technology", e-mail
    to Robert Silvestri, 18 Nov. 2000.

c) **A work of art**
    When the work of art has been reproduced in a book, state the
    artist's name, the title of the artwork, the institution or private
    owner of the work, the city where it is located, and the page, slide,
    figure or plate number by which it is designated in the source.

    [6]Michelangelo, *The Rondanini Pietà*, Museo del Castello
    Sforzesco, Milan. *Testament: The Bible as History*, by John Romer
    (New York: Holt, 1988) plate 38.

    When the work of art is viewed in its original form or found in an
    unpublished source, give the artist's name, the name of the work
    (italicized), the name of the institution housing the artwork, and
    the location.

    [7]Rosa Bonheur, *Plowing Scene*, Museum of Fine Arts,
    Boston.

d) **Film**
    In general, the information most relevant to your textual reference
    is given first (the name of the film or the song, the director or the
    producer of a performance, etc.).

Reference to film itself

[8]*Vertigo*, prod. Herbert Coleman and Alfred Hitchcock, dir. Alfred Hitchcock, Paramount, 1959.

Reference to director

[9]Atom Egoyan, dir., *The Sweet Hereafter*, Alliance Communications, 1997.

e) **Television program**

Reference to program itself

[10]"Land of the Eagle," *Nature*, PBS, WNED, Buffalo, NY, 3 May 1992.

Reference to actor

[11]Martin Sheen, actor, *The West Wing*, NBC, CTV, Toronto, 25 Apr. 2001.

f) **Sound recording**

Reference to lyrics
[12]David Byrne, "The Big Country," *The Talking Heads: More Songs about Buildings and Food*, Sire, 9147-6058, 1978.

Reference to producer

[13]Phil Spector, prod., *Let It Be*, The Beatles, Apple, SW-6386, 1970.

g) **Videotape/DVD**

[14]*Science Study Skills, Section Two: Science Labs*, prod. Ann Wetmore and Christine Shelton, videotape, Mount Saint Vincent University Student Affairs Dept., 1991.

[15]*Lawrence of Arabia*, dir. David Lean, DVD, Columbia Tristar, 2001 [1962].

h) Live performance

[16]*The Millionairess*, by Bernard Shaw, dir. Allen MacInnis, Shaw Festival, Niagara-on-the-Lake, 23 May 2001.

i) CD-ROM
For an article located on a CD-ROM, give the author's name and the title of the article, along with the full publication details of both the periodical (where appropriate) and the CD-ROM itself. Otherwise, cite only the details of the CD-ROM.

[19]Abby Ellin, "Online Teaching: the Battle in Cyberspace," *New York Times* 6 Aug. 2000, *New York Times Ondisc*, CD-ROM (UMI-Proquest, 2000).

[20]*Time Management for Students*, CD-ROM (Toronto: York University, 1999).

j) Software

[21]*WordPerfect Office 2000*, Computer Software (Corel Corporation, 1999).

Documenting Online Sources
The principles of documentation described previously apply also to material obtained using the Internet or other electronic sources.

Here is an in-text reference:

According to *The Internet Encyclopedia of Philosophy*, utilitarians argue that capital punishment "prevents the criminal from repeating his crime . . . [and] deters crime by discouraging would-be offenders."[1]

Here is the corresponding note, which includes the date on which the page was accessed:

[1]"Capital Punishment," *The Internet Encyclopedia of Philosophy*, ed. James Fieser and Brad Dowden, U of Tennessee at Martin, 2 June 2000 < http://www.utm.edu/research/iep/c/capitalp.htm >.

If you make any subsequent reference to this article, you could use a shortened form in the note, a form that includes enough information to identify the work:

[9] "Capital."

The anatomy of a typical footnote for an internet source is given in the box below:

> [1]**Web page author (if known), "web page title,"** *web site title*, **editors (if known), date of creation, web site sponsor, date of access, <internet address (URL)>.**

Following are sample notes:

a) **Complete online scholarly projects, reference databases, or professional or personal sites**

[1]*The History of the Book in Canada Project*, ed. Patricia Fleming and Yvan Lamonde, 7 Feb. 2000, U of Toronto Library, 2 June 2000 < http://www.hbic.library.utoronto.ca >.

[2]*The Sixties Project*, Coordinator Kali Tal, 28 Jan. 1999, Institute for Advanced Technology in the Humanities (IATH), U of Virginia at Charlottesville, 2 June 2000 < http://lists.village.virginia.edu/sixties/ >.

[3] *Early Modern English Dictionaries Database*, ed. Ian Lancashire, Oct. 1999, U of Toronto, 8 June 2000 < http://www.chass.utoronto.ca/english/emed/emedd.html >.

[4] *SSHRC Home Page*, 30 June 2000, Social Sciences and Humanities Research Council, 2 July 2000 < http://www. sshrc.ca/english/index.html >.

[5] *Ontario Ministry of Education Home Page*, 3 July 2000, Ontario Ministry of Education, Training, Colleges, and Universities, 3 July 2000 < http://www.edu.gov.on.ca /eng/welcome.html >.

[6] Christopher A. Long, Home Page, 8 June 2000 < http://www.users.dircon.co.uk/long/ >.

[7] Henry Churchyard, *Jane Austen Information Page*, 8 June 2000 < http://www.pemberley.com/janeinfo/janeinfo.html >.

b) **An article, poem, or short story within a scholarly project, database, or site**

[8] "Austria," *Encyclopaedia Britannica Online*, Encyclopaedia Britannica, 3 July 2000 < http://search.eb.com/bol/topic? eu = 117981&sctn = 2 >.

[9] "Capital Punishment," *The Internet Encyclopedia of Philosophy*, ed. James Fieser and Brad Dowden, U of Tennessee at Martin, 2 June 2000 < http://www.utm.edu/research/iep/ c/capitalp.htm >.

[10] Margaret Avison, "The Swimmer's Moment," *Winter Sun*, 1962, *Canadian Poetry*, ed. Ian Lancashire, Sophie Kaszuba, and Sian Meikle, U of Toronto English Library, 8 June 2000 < http://www/library.utoronto.ca/canpoetry/avison/ poem7.htm >.

[11]Gerard Manley Hopkins, "The Windhover," *Poems*, 1918, *Representative Poetry On-line*, vers. 2.07, ed. Ian Lancashire. U of Toronto, 8 June 2000 < http://www.library.utoronto.ca/utel/ rp/poems/hopkins4.html >.

[12]Elizabeth Gaskell, "French Life," *The Gaskell Web*, ed. Mitsuharu Matsuoka, 30 May 2000, Nagoya U, Japan, 8 June 2000 < http://lang.nagoya-u.ac.jp/matsuoka/EG-Life.html >.

c) **An electronic book**

[13]Lucy Maud Montgomery, *Anne's House of Dreams* (New York: Gosset and Dunlap, 1917), *The Electronic Text Center*, ed. Jennifer Easley, June 1998, Alderman Lib., U of Virginia, 3 July 2000 < http://etext.lib.virginia.edu/toc/public/MonAnne. html >.

d) **An article in a scholarly journal**

[14]Richard Danson Brown, "A 'goodlie bridge' between the Old and the New: the transformation of complaint in Spenser's The Ruines of Time," *Renaissance Forum* 2.1 (1997): 64 pars., 8 June 2000 < http://www.hull.ac.uk/renforum/v2no1/brown. htm >.

[15]Ian Buchanan, "Deleuze and Pop Music," *Australian Humanities Review* 7 (August-October 1997): 24 pars., 2 June 2000 < http://www.lib.latrobe.edu.au/AHR/archive?Issur-August-1997-buchanan.html >.

e) **An article in a magazine**

[16]Kevin Hunt, "The Cultural Currency of the Book," *CMC Magazine* Aug. 1998, 1 July 2000 < http://www.december.com/ cmc/mag/1998/aug/hunt.html >.

f) An article in a newspaper or on a newswire
In both examples the date of creation and the date of access are the
same: 3 July 2000. The date of access comes after the creation
date.

[17]Stephen Kinzer, "A Race to Save Roman Splendors From
Drowning," *New York Times on the Web* 3 July 2000, 3 July 2000.
< http://www.nytimes.com/library/world/europe/
070300turkey-roman.html >.

[18]James McCarten, "Consider splitting up gasoline retailers
and refiners, Ontario task force to tell Ottawa," *CP Online* 3
July 2000, 3 July 2000 < http://www.calgaryplus.ca/cponline/
news/ >.

g) A review

[19]Jean-Jacques Malo, rev. of *From Hanoi to Hollywood: The
Vietnam War in American Film*, by Linda Dittmar and Gene
Michaud, *Viet Nam Generation Journal and Newsletter* 4.1-2
(1992): 12 pars., 2 June 2000 < http://lists.village.virginia.
edu/sixties/HTML_docs/Texts/Reviews?Malo_Hanoi
_Hollywood.html >.

[20]Christopher E. Forth, rev. of *Leisure Settings: Bourgeois
Culture, Medicine and the Spa in Modern France*, by Douglas Peter
Mackaman, *H-France, H-Net Reviews* Oct. 1999, 6 June 2000
< http://www/h-net.msu.edu/reviews/showrev.cgi?path=
25602940965000 >.

h) An abstract

[21]Nelda Swinton, "The Inuit Sea Goddess," *Concordia
University Art History Theses Abstracts On-line*, abstract, 3 July
2000 < http://art-history.concordia.ca/RVACanada/abstracts/
swinton.html >.

[22]Franklin Griffiths, "Canada as a Sovereign State," *Canadian Foreign Policy Journal* 2.1 (Spring 1994), abstract, 3 July 2000 < http://temagami.carleton.ca/npsia/cfpj/fabstracts/fv2.1.html# Griffiths >.

i) **An editorial**

Again, the date of creation is listed before the date of access, and both dates happen to be the same in the example.

[23]"Do you know me?" editorial, *Globe and Mail* 3 July 2000, 3 July 2000 < http://www.globeandmail.ca/gam/Editorials/20000703/ECELEB.html >.

j) **A letter to the editor**

[24]Ulana Winter, "Low marks for history quiz," letter, *Globe and Mail* 3 July 2000, 3 July 2000. < http://www.globeandmail.ca/gam/Letters/20000703/MOLETS-4.html >.

k) **A government document**

[25]Canadian Heritage, *Culture and heritage: Making room for Canada's voices* (Ottawa: Canadian Heritage, 1999), 5 July 2000 < http://www.pch.gc.ca/culture/report/HTM/1.htm >.

l) **A work of art**

[26]Paul Cézanne, *Still Life with Apples and a Pot of Primroses*, 1890, Metropolitan Museum of Art, New York, 12 July 2000 < http://www.metmuseum.org/collections/images/ep/images/ep51.112.1.R.jpg >.

m) **A map**

[27]*Paris, France*, map, US Dept. of State, 1985, 12 July 2000 < http://www.lib.utexas.edu/Libs/PCL/Map_collection/ world_cities/Paris.jpg >.

n) **A web discussion posting**

[28]Stephen L. Keck, "Lady Travellers in the Empire," online posting, 5 Mar.1999, H-Albion, 13 July 2000 < http://www2. h-net.msu.edu/ ~ albion/ >.

o) **A listserv message**

[29]Leofranc Holford-Strevens, "Re: Socrates' date of birth and death," online posting, 16 Dec. 1999, Classicists, 12 July 2000 < http://listserv.liv.ac.uk/archives/classicists.html >.

p) **A newsgroup message**

[30]Jonathan Brown, "Karl Muck's Wagner recordings," online posting, 1 Aug. 2000, 2 Aug. 2000 < news:humanities.music. composers.wagner >.

q) **A real-time communication**

[31]Karen Taylor, online discussion, 1 Aug. 2000, Tapped In, 1 Aug. 2000 < telnet://tappedin.sri.com: 7777 >.

74

Bibliography

If you are using the footnoting method of documentation, you must title your list of references **Bibliography**. A bibliography lists all the works consulted during the research of an essay, even those to which no reference is made in the essay.

Guidelines:

- Entries are arranged alphabetically by author's last name on a separate page, entitled "Bibliography," at the end of the essay.

- The page or pages should be numbered in sequence with the pages of the essay.

- Double-spacing is used within and between entries.

- The first line of each entry begins flush with the left margin, and subsequent lines are indented five spaces.

- The entries have three main divisions, each separated by a period: the author's name, the title, and the publishing information.

- If two or more works by the same author are to be listed, alphabetize the works by title, then give the author's name in the first entry. For additional entries type three unspaced hyphens and a period instead of the author's name; leave one space and type the title. (See examples that follow.)

- When arranging several works by the same first author, single-author entries precede multiple-author entries. Multiple-author entries with the same first author and different subsequent authors are arranged alphabetically.

- Publishers' names are shortened. Only the important, identifying words are necessary. Eliminate words like "limited," "books," "company," etc. For example, R.R. Bowker Co. becomes Bowker. University Press is designated by UP. For example, University of Toronto Press becomes U of Toronto P.

Bibliographic entries: Examples
In general, an entry must contain information about author, title, and publication data. Following are three sample entries: one for a section of a book, one for an article in a periodical, and one for a second work by the same author. Notice the differences in punctuation from that used in the footnote or endnote.

Sample Entry: Article in a Book

> Flintstone, Fred, Barney Rubble, and Betty Rubble. "Ode to Wilma." *The Rock Chronicles: The Collected Works of Fred Flinstone.* Ed. Arnold A. Anthropologist. 2nd ed. Vol. 4. Prehistoric Verse 17. New York: Cambrian P, 2000. 17-20.

Sample Entry: Article in a Periodical

> Rubble, Fred, and Betty Rubble. "The Ballad of Fred and Wilma." *Journal of the Prehistoric Family* 23.3 (2000): 18-69.

Sample Entry: Second Work by Same Author

> ---. "Postmodern Perspectives on Fred and Wilma." *Journal of the Prehistoric Family* 24.1 (2001): 5-22.

Each of the examples used in "How to Footnote/Endnote" is presented below in the form appropriate for a bibliography. Each entry is labelled in bold. Find and follow the examples which most closely conform to the sources you are dealing with. Remember, all types of entries conform to the basic patterns exemplified above.

Bibliography

Books

a) **A book with a single author**

> Chittick, Kathryn. *Dickens and the 1830s.* Cambridge: Cambridge UP, 1990.

When there are two or more works by the same author, use the following format. Titles should be arranged in alphabetical order.

Daiches, David. *Critical Approaches to Literature*. Englewood Cliffs, NJ: Prentice-Hall, 1956.

---. *Milton*. New York: Norton Library-Norton, 1966.

b) **A book with an editor or translator**

Dickens, Charles. *The Personal History of David Copperfield*. Ed. Trevor Blount. Harmondsworth, England: Penguin, 1966.

Menander. *Plays and Fragments*. Trans. Norma Miller. London: Penguin, 1987.

c) **A book with an editor or translator, when references are to the edited material**

Blount, Trevor, ed. *The Personal History of David Copperfield*. By Charles Dickens. Harmondsworth, England: Penguin, 1966.

Miller, Norma, trans. *Plays and Fragments*. By Menander. London: Penguin, 1987.

d) **A book with two or more authors**

Two or three authors: list all authors
Malcolmson, Patrick, and Richard Myers. *The Canadian Regime*. Peterborough, ON: Broadview P, 1996.

Fleet, Joan, Fiona Goodchild, and Richard Zajchowski. *Learning for Success: Skills and Strategies for Canadian Students*. Toronto: Harcourt Brace, 1994.

Four or more authors: list only the first author
Belenky, Mary Field, et al. *Women's Ways of Knowing: The Development of Self, Voice, and Mind.* New York: Basic, 1986.

e) **A book with a corporate author**

Canadian Historical Association. *Regionalism in the Canadian Community 1867-1967.* Ed. Mason Wade. Toronto: U of Toronto P, 1969.

f) **A book with no author given**

1990 Stoddart Restaurant Guide to Toronto. Toronto: Stoddart, 1990.

g) **An edition other than the first**
The edition can also be noted by year or name (e.g., 2000 ed., rev. ed.).

Strath, Lucille, Heather Avery, and Karen Taylor. *Notes on the Preparation of Essays in the Arts and Sciences.* 4th ed. Peterborough, ON: Academic Skills Centre, Trent U, 1993.

h) **A work in several volumes**
If all the volumes to which you are referring have the same title, the number of volumes is placed immediately before the publishing information.

Weber, Max. *Economy and Society: An Outline of Interpretive Sociology.* Ed. Guenther Roth and Claus Wittich. Trans. Ephraim Fischoff, et al. 3 vols. New York: Bedminster, 1968.

If the volume you have used has a title that is different from the title of the entire collection, give the title of the single volume first. Then, after citing publication details, indicate which volume you have used, followed by the multivolume title.

Ehrenpreis, Irvin. *Dean Swift*. London: Methuen, 1983. Vol. 3 of
Swift: The Man, His Works, and the Age. 3 vols. 1969-83.

i) **A book in a series**

Pratt, Louis H. *Alice Malsenior Walker: an Annotated
Bibliography, 1968-1986*. Meckler's Studies and
Bibliographies on Black Americans 1. Westport, CT:
Meckler, 1988.

j) **A book with a publisher's imprint**
The name of the publisher's imprint can be found on the title page
usually above the publisher's name. The imprint (here, Borzoi) is
given before the name of the publisher (here, Knopf), and the
names are joined with a hyphen.

Bettelheim, Bruno. *The Uses of Enchantment: The Meaning and
Importance of Fairy Tales*. New York: Borzoi-Knopf, 1976.

k) **A republished book**
When a book has been republished, give the date of the original
publication before the publication information.

Traill, Catharine Parr. *The Backwoods of Canada*. Ed. Michael
Peterman. Centre for Editing Early Canadian Texts 11.
1846. Ottawa: Carleton UP, 1997.

Sections of Books

a) **One part of a book by a single author (e.g., poem, short story,
essay, article, or chapter)**

LaViolette, Forest E. "The Potlatch Law: Wardship and
Enforcement." *The Struggle for Survival: Indian Cultures and
the Protestant Ethic in British Columbia*. Toronto: U of
Toronto P, 1973. 44-97.

b) **An article in a book in which there are articles by a number of writers**

Weiler, Kathleen. "You've Got to Stay There and Fight: Sex
     Equity, Schooling, and Work." *Changing Education: Women
     as Radicals and Conservators.* Ed. Joyce Antler and Sari
     Knopp Bilen. Albany, NY: SUNY P, 1990. 217-36.

c) **A work in an anthology**
    If the work is a short poem, short story, or essay (in other words, a
    work that has probably not been previously published on its own),
    enclose the title of this work in quotation marks. In the example,
    1948 is the page on which the poem is found, not a date.

Yeats, W.B. "The Second Coming." *The Norton Anthology of
     English Literature.* Ed. M.H. Abrams. 5th ed. Vol. 2. New
     York: Norton, 1986. 1948.

If the work is a play, novel, or long poem (in other words, a work
that has probably been previously published on its own), italicize
the title of this work.

Shakespeare, William. *Hamlet. William Shakespeare: The Complete
     Works.* Ed. Alfred Harbage. Baltimore: Penguin, 1969. 930-
     76.

d) **An introduction, preface, foreword, or afterword**

Lindenberger, Herbert. Foreword. *MLA Style Manual and Guide
     to Scholarly Publishing.* By Joseph Gibaldi. 2nd ed. New
     York: MLA, 1998. xvi-xvii.

e) **An article in a reference book (encyclopaedia, dictionary)**
    If the article has an author, begin with that author's name.
    (Remember that in reference books, authorship is often indicated
    only by initials, usually given at the close of an article. If the
    author's name is abbreviated to initials, find the key to

abbreviations or the list of contributing authors, and give the author's full name in your citation.)

Cairns, Julia. "Spry, Constance." *Dictionary of National Biography 1951-1960.* 1971 ed.

If there is no author indicated, begin with the title of the article. Only the year of publication need be given for well-known multivolume reference books.

"Axminster Carpets." *Encyclopaedia Britannica: Micropaedia.* 1974.

Articles in Periodicals (journals, magazines, newspapers)

a) **Journal articles**

    An article published in a journal with continuous pagination throughout the annual volume
    Identify the volume number (83) but not the issue number.

    Bynum, David E. "Themes of the Young Hero in Serbocroatian Oral Epic Tradition." *PMLA* 83 (1968): 1295-303.

    An article from a journal that paginates each issue separately
    Identify the volume number (19) and the issue number (4).

    Dosman, Edgar J. "Hemispheric Relations in the 1980s: A Perspective from Canada." *Journal of Canadian Studies* 19.4 (1984): 42-60.

b) **A magazine article**
    If the magazine is published monthly, the month may be listed without the day. The names of all the months are abbreviated with the exceptions of May, June, and July.

    Fulford, Robert. "Regarding Alex Colville." *Saturday Night* 17 June 2000: 30-34.

c) **A newspaper article**
Give the name of the newspaper without the word "the," e.g., *Globe and Mail*, not *The Globe and Mail*. When the place of publication is not part of the newspaper's title, it is added in square brackets after the title. When the newspaper has different editions, the name of the edition that appears on the masthead is placed after the date and preceded by a comma.

McCarthy, Shawn. "Clock now ticking on free-trade deal." *Globe and Mail* [Toronto] 23 Apr. 2001, metro ed.: A1.

If the name of the author is not given, begin with the title of the article.

"Wal-Mart heir ousts Gates as world's richest man." *National Post* [Toronto] 23 Apr. 2001: A2.

d) **An editorial or a letter to the editor**

"Making it a Summit for all the Americas." Editorial. *Globe & Mail* [Toronto] 23 Apr. 2001: A18.

Theresa Manchester. Letter. *National Post* [Toronto] 23 Apr. 2001: A15.

Aaron Edison. Letter. *Atlantic.* Feb. 2000: 69.

e) **A review (of a book, movie, or live performance)**
The phrase "rev. of" is used to introduce the material being reviewed.

Cottrell, Robert. "Founding Father." Rev. of *My Six Years with Gorbachev*, by Anatoly S. Chernyaev. *The New York Review of Books* 26 Apr. 2001: 20-22.

For a performance review, add the relevant production information, such as place of performance and name of performing company.

Franklin, Nancy. "Blarney Stones." Rev. of *Stones in his Pockets*, by Marie Jones. Golden Theatre, New York. *The New Yorker* 16 Apr. 2001: 88-89.

If the review has no title, place "rev. of" immediately after the name of the reviewer:

Phelp, Jenefer. Rev. of *Input, Interaction and the Second Language Learner*, by Susan M. Gass. *Language Awareness* 9 (2000):115-17.

Other Sources

a) **A government document**
When no author is given, the government body is treated as the author. The name of the government author is followed by the title of the document, italicized. When title pages are given in more than one language, only one version need be used. After the title, the available relevant publication information is given (publisher, place and date of publication, pages, etc.). Citing government documents can be complicated, but the government documents librarian or another member of the library staff will be able to help you.

Ontario Legislative Assembly. Standing Committee on Social Development. *Report on Food Banks*. 2nd session. 34th Parliament. Toronto: Government of Ontario, May 1983.

b) **A dissertation or thesis**

Unpublished

Niero, Christine. "Making Stories: Studies in Contemporary Canadian Metafiction." Diss. Queen's U, 1987.

Published

Finley, A.G. *Shipbuilding in St. Martins 1840-1880: A Case Study of Family Enterprise on the Fundy Shore.* M.A. thesis. U of New Brunswick, 1980 Ottawa: Canadian Theses on Microfiche, 1984. 47732.

c) **A pamphlet**

Treat a pamphlet as you would a book. Often, publication details will be sketchy: use n.p. for "no known publisher" or "no known place of publication," n. pag. for "no pagination," and n.d. for "no date given" to indicate missing data.

Human Rights: What to Do about Discrimination or Harassment. Peterborough, ON: Trent U, n.d.

d) **Archival material**

The format for citing archival material varies; however, certain pieces of standard information are necessary in all archival citations. The citation must first enable the reader to locate the archival material by identifying the repository and the material's location within the repository; it must also describe the material as any citation would, giving author, date, etc. The National Archives of Canada is abbreviated NAC. RG stands for Record Group (the collection in the NAC where the material may be found). The material cited here can be located on pages 131 and 132 of volume 1846.

NAC R10. Vol. 1846. 131, 132. "Treaty No. 3 between Her Majesty the Queen and the Saulteaux Tribe of the Ojibbeway Indians at the Northwest Angle of the Lake of the Woods with Adhesions, 3 October 1873."

e) **A legal document/court case**

In general, a citation of a legal document must include the following: identification of case or document, date of document, and information making clear where the document can be found (name, volume, and page of court report, for example). The example below refers to a case brought before the Supreme Court of Canada.

Law Society of British Columbia v. Andrews. 1989. 1 S.C.R.

f) Material from an information service

Cite the material from the service in much the same way as you would cite other printed material, giving the publication information. Add the name of the service and the file number at the end of the entry.

Limbrick, Liddy, et al. *Peer-Power: Using Peer Tutoring to Help Low-Progress Readers in Primary and Secondary Schools.* Wellington: New Zealand Council for Educational Research, 1985. 10. ERIC ED 326 858.

If the material has not been published previously, cite the service as the publisher. No place of publication is needed. Retain the file number at the end of the citation.

Thomas, Susan B. "Concerns About Gifted Children: A Paper and Abstract Bibliography." ERIC, 1974. ERIC ED 091 083.

g) An advertisement

Nissan. "Introducing the new Infiniti QX4." Advertisement. *The New Yorker* 24 Apr. 2000: 2-5.

Non-print material

a) A lecture, address, debate

If the title of the presentation is not known, use an accurate descriptive word (e.g., Lecture, Address, Debate). Do not italicize this word or place it in quotation marks.

Syrett, John. "Nixon the Great Before Watergate." Hist. 312.
Trent U, 7 Mar. 2000.

Neufeld, James, Zailig Pollock, and Suzanne Bailey. Debate.
Engl. 205. Trent U, 26 Mar. 2001.

b) **A personal communication (interview, letter)**
Give the name of the person contacted, the appropriate descriptive
label (e.g., Personal Interview, Telephone Interview, Personal
Letter), and the date.

O'Donoghue, Judith A. Personal Interview. 9 Apr. 2001.

For e-mail communications, follow this format:

May, Nadine. "Re: Conference Paper." E-mail to the author. 11
May 2001.

Walker, Mike. "Learning Disabilities: Technology." E-mail to
Robert Silvestri. 18 Nov. 2000.

c) **A work of art**
When the work of art has been reproduced in a book, state the
artist's name, the title of the artwork, the institution or private
owner of the work, the city where it is located, and the page, slide,
figure or plate number by which it is designated in the source.

Michelangelo. *The Rondanini Pietà*. Museo del Castello
Sforzesco, Miilan. *Testament: The Bible as History*. By John
Romer. New York: Holt, 1988. Plate 38.

When the work of art is viewed in its original form or found in an
unpublished source, give the artist's name, the name of the work
italicized, the name of the institution housing the artwork, and the
location.

Bonheur, Rosa. *Plowing Scene*. Museum of Fine Arts, Boston.

d) **Film**

Reference to film itself

Vertigo. Prod. Herbert Coleman and Alfred Hitchcock. Dir.
Alfred Hitchcock. Paramount, 1959.

Reference to director

Egoyan, Atom, dir. *The Sweet Hereafter.* Alliance
Communications, 1997.

e) **Television program**

Reference to program itself

"Land of the Eagle." *Nature.* PBS. WNED, Buffalo, NY. 3 May
1992.

Reference to actor

Sheen, Martin, actor. *The West Wing.* NBC. CTV, Toronto, ON.
25 Apr. 2001.

f) **Sound recording**

Reference to lyrics

Byrne, David. "The Big Country." *The Talking Heads: More Songs
about Buildings and Food.* Sire, 9147-6058, 1978.

Reference to producer

Spector, Phil, prod. *Let It Be.* The Beatles. Apple, SW-6386, 1970.

g) **Videotape/DVD**

Science Study Skills, Section Two: Science Labs. Prod. Ann
   Wetmore and Christine Shelton. Videotape. Mount Saint
   Vincent University Student Affairs Dept., 1991.

Lawrence of Arabia. Dir. David Lean. DVD. 1962. Columbia
   Tristar, 2001.

h) **Live performance**

The Millionairess. By Bernard Shaw. Dir. Allen MacInnis. Shaw
   Festival, Niagara-on-the-Lake. 23 May 2001.

i) **CD-ROM**

Ellin, Abby. "Online Teaching: the Battle in Cyberspace." *New
   York Times* 6 Aug. 2000. *New York Times Ondisc*. CD-ROM.
   UMI-Proquest, 2000.

Time Management for Students. CD-ROM. Toronto: York
   University, 1999.

j) **Software**

WordPerfect Office 2000. Computer Software. Corel
   Corporation, 1999.

Online Sources

The main difference between a citation of a printed text, such as a
book, and a web document is the substitution of internet source data for
publication data. In other words, instead of listing the name of the
publisher and the place and year of publication, an internet source is
documented in terms of its internet address (URL or other source), its
date of publication on the Internet (if available), and the date on which
you accessed it.

88

The anatomy of a typical internet citation for a bibliography is given in the box below.

> **Author's Name.** *Document Title.* **Date of Internet Publication. Date of Access <Internet Address>.**
>
> Flintstone, Fred. *Bedrock Ballads.* 4 Jan. 1998. 21 July 2000 <http://www. bedrocku/fflintstone/ballads.html>.

a) **Complete online scholarly projects, reference databases, or professional or personal sites**

The History of the Book in Canada Project. Ed. Patricia Fleming and Yvan Lamonde. 7 Feb. 2000. U of Toronto Library. 2 June 2000 < http://www.hbic.library.utoronto.ca >.

The Sixties Project. Coordinator Kali Tal. 28 Jan. 1999. Institute for Advanced Technology in the Humanities (IATH), U of Virginia at Charlottesville. 2 June 2000 < http://lists.village. virginia.edu/sixties/ >.

Early Modern English Dictionaries Database. Ed. Ian Lancashire. Oct. 1999. U of Toronto. 8 June 2000 < http://www.chass. utoronto.ca/english/emed/emedd.html >.

SSHRC Home Page. 30 June 2000. Social Sciences and Humanities Research Council. 2 July 2000 < http://www.sshrc.ca/ english/index.html >.

Ontario Ministry of Education Home Page. 3 July 2000. Ontario Ministry of Education, Training, Colleges, and Universities. 3 July 2000 < http://www.edu.gov.on.ca/eng/welcome. html >.

Long, Christopher A. Home Page. 8 June 2000
   < http://www.users.dircon.co.uk/ ~calong/index.
   html >.

Churchyard, Henry. *Jane Austen Information Page*. 8 June
   < http://www.pemberley.com/janeinfo/ janeinfo. ht

b) **An article, poem, or short story within a scholarly project, database, or site**

"Austria." *Encyclopaedia Britannica Online*. Encyclopaedia
   Britannica. 3 July 2000 < http://search.eb.com/bol/
   topic?eu = 117981&sctn = 2 >.

"Capital Punishment." *The Internet Encyclopedia of Philosophy*.
   Ed. James Fieser and Brad Dowden. U of Tennessee at
   Martin. 2 June 2000 < http://www.utm.edu/research/iep/
   c/capitalp.htm >.

Avison, Margaret. "The Swimmer's Moment." *Winter Sun*. 1962.
   Canadian Poetry. Ed. Ian Lancashire, Sophie Kaszuba, and
   Sian Meikle. U of Toronto English Library. 8 June 2000
   < http://www/library.utoronto.ca/canpoetry/avison/
   poem7.htm >.

Hopkins, Gerard Manley. "The Windhover." *Poems*. 1918.
   Representative Poetry On-line. Vers. 2.07. Ed. Ian Lancashire.
   U of Toronto. 8 June 2000 < http://www.library.
   utoronto.ca/utel/rp/poems/hopkins4.html >.

Gaskell, Elizabeth. "French Life." *The Gaskell Web*. Ed.
   Mitsuharu Matsuoka. 30 May 2000. Nagoya U, Japan. 8 June
   2000 < http://lang.nagoya-u.ac.jp/matsuoka/EG-Life.
   html >.

c) **An electronic book**

> Montgomery, Lucy Maud. *Anne's House of Dreams*. New York:
> Gosset and Dunlap, 1917. *The Electronic Text Center*. Ed.
> Jennifer Easley. June 1998. Alderman Lib., U of Virginia. 3
> July 2000 < http://etext.lib.virginia.edu/toc/public/
> MonAnne.html >.

d) **An article in a scholarly journal**

> Brown, Richard Danson. "A 'goodlie bridge' between the Old
> and the New: the transformation of complaint in Spenser's
> The Ruines of Time." *Renaissance Forum* 2.1 (1997): 64 pars.
> 8 June 2000 < http://www.hull.ac.uk/renforum/v2no1/
> brown.htm >.

> Buchanan, Ian. "Deleuze and Pop Music." *Australian Humanities
> Review* 7 (August-October 1997): 24 pars. 2 June 2000
> < http://www.lib.latrobe.edu.au/AHRarchive?Issur-
> August-1997-buchanan.html >.

e) **An article in a magazine**

> Hunt, Kevin. "The Cultural Currency of the Book." *CMC
> Magazine* Aug. 1998. 1 July 2000 < http://www.
> december.com/cmc/mag/1998/aug/hunt.html >.

f) **An article in a newspaper or on a newswire**

> Kinzer, Stephen. "A Race to Save Roman Splendors From
> Drowning." *New York Times on the Web* 3 July 2000. 3 July
> 2000 < http://www.nytimes.com/library/world/europe/
> 070300turkey-roman.html >.

McCarten, James. "Consider splitting up gasoline retailers and refiners, Ontario task force to tell Ottawa." *CP Online* 3 July 2000. 3 July 2000 < http://www.calgaryplus.ca/cponline/news/ >.

g) **A review**

Malo, Jean-Jacques. Rev. of *From Hanoi to Hollywood: The Vietnam War in American Film*, by Linda Dittmar and Gene Michaud. *Viet Nam Generation Journal and Newsletter* 4.1-2 (1992): 12 pars. 2 June 2000 < http://lists.village.virginia. edu/sixties/HTML_docs/Texts/Reviews?Malo_Hanoi_ Hollywood.html >.

Forth, Christopher E. Rev. of *Leisure Settings: Bourgeois Culture, Medicine and the Spa in Modern France*, by Douglas Peter Mackaman. *H-France, H-Net Reviews* Oct. 1999. 6 June 2000 < http://www/h-net.msu.edu/reviews/showrevcgi? path=25602940965000 >.

h) **An abstract**

Swinton, Nelda. "The Inuit Sea Goddess." *Concordia University Art History Theses Abstracts On-line.* Abstract. 3 July 2000 < http://art-history.concordia.ca/RVACanada/abstracts/ swinton.html >.

Griffiths, Franklin. "Canada as a Sovereign State." *Canadian Foreign Policy Journal* 2.1 (Spring 1994). Abstract. 3 July 2000 < http://temagami.carleton.ca/npsia/cfpj/fabstracts/ fv2.1.html#Griffiths >.

i) **An editorial**

"Do you know me?" Editorial. *Globe and Mail* 3 July 2000. 3 July
    2000 < http://www.globeandmail.ca/gam/Editorials/
    20000703/ECELEB.html >.

j) **A letter to the editor**

Winter, U. "Low marks for history quiz." Letter. *Globe and Mail*
    3 July 2000. 3 July 2000 < http://www.globeandmail.ca/
    gam/Letters/20000703/MOLETS-4.html >.

k) **A government document**

Canadian Heritage. *Culture and heritage: Making room for
    Canada's voices.* Ottawa: Canadian Heritage, 1999. 5 July
    2000 < http://www.pch.gc.ca/culture/report/HTM/
    1.htm >.

l) **A work of art**

Cézanne, Paul. *Still Life with Apples and a Pot of Primroses.* 1890.
    Metropolitan Museum of Art, New York. 12 July 2000
    < http://www.metmuseum.org/collections/images/ep/
    images/ep51.112.1.R.jpg >.

m) **A map**

Paris, France. Map. US Dept. of State, 1985. 12 July 2000
    < http://www.lib.utexas.edu/Libs/PCL/Map_collection/
    world_cities/Paris.jpg >.

n) **A web discussion posting**

> Keck, Stephen L. "Lady Travellers in the Empire." Online
> posting. 5 Mar. 1999. H-Albion. 13 July 2000
> < http://www2.h-net.msu.edu/ ~ albion/ >.

TIPS & NOTES

Discussion postings often have very complex
URLs because they are found and displayed
through search engines. The complete address
for Keck's posting, for example, is
<http://h-net.msu.edu/cgi-bin/logbrowse.pl?
trx=vx&list=h-albion&month=9903&week=a
&msg=uT48xt4s3Cjzl2n9Ip%2b3nQ&user=&
pw=>. The URL listed in the sample citation
is for the general H-Albion discussion group.

---

o) **A listserv message**

> Holford-Strevens, Leofranc. "Re: Socrates' date of birth and
> death." Online posting. 16 Dec. 1999. Classicists. 12 July
> 2000 < http://listserv.liv.ac.uk/archives/classicists.html >.

p) **A newsgroup message**

> Brown, Jonathan. "Karl Muck's Wagner recordings." Online
> posting. 1 Aug. 2000. 2 Aug. 2000 < news:humanities.
> music.composers.wagner >.

q) **A real-time communication**

> Taylor, Karen. Online discussion. 1 Aug. 2000. Tapped In. 1
> Aug. 2000 < telnet://tappedin.sri.com: 7777 >.

94

For an alphabetical listing of all the sources described in this section in the form of a Bibliography or Works Cited list, see pp. 99-106.

Method Two: Parenthetical Documentation Style A (MLA)

This method of documentation is based on the guidelines set by the Modern Language Association (MLA). It is most commonly used in **the humanities**, especially in **English literature** and **philosophy**. It is also preferred for many interdisciplinary essays where the nature of the focus is close to philosophy or English literature, in **cultural studies, native studies,** and **women's studies,** for example. See Part III-C (pp. 137-62) for preferred documentation styles for each discipline.

How to Use Parenthetical Documentation Style A

1. **Citing authors' names**

a) Whenever an idea, piece of information, or quotation from one of your sources appears in the essay, you insert, next to the item needing documentation, the author's name and the relevant page number(s) in parentheses.

> *Example*:
> Policy during the Milner era denied the Africans, Asians, and coloured people access to full citizenship (Davenport 152).

Note that the reference does not contain any punctuation or abbreviation for the word "page" or "pages." Name and page number are separated by a single space.

b) Place the parenthetical reference close to the material it documents, preferably at the end of the sentence.

2. **Citing works by more than one author or with no author**

a) If you are citing a source which has two or three authors, include all the authors' names.

> *Example*:
> (Langer and Zasloff 1)

If there are four or more authors, use the first author's name and "et al.," which means "and others."

Example:
(Belenky et al. 42-64)

b) If you are citing a work which has no author or which is listed by title in your works cited list, give the title or a shortened version of it in the parenthetical reference.

Example:
A recent article in the *Globe and Mail* notes that budget cuts to Statistics Canada will result in fewer facts about science and technology being available to Canadians ("Ottawa Cuts" B4).

b) **Specifying the location of a source**

a) A page number alone will not always identify the location of a source. If you are citing a multivolume work, you must also include the relevant volume number.

Example:
(Weber 3: 141)

b) In references to works of literature, it is often preferable to specify location by some designation other than page number—for example, act, scene, and line, or stanza, canto or book. Avoid abbreviations except when they are necessary to establish what the numbers designate. Use Arabic numerals (unless your instructor prefers Roman numerals).

Example: The reference indicates that the passage quoted appears in act 3, scene 2, lines 73-75 of the play.

> Give me that man
> That is not passion's slave, and I will wear him
> In my heart's core, ay, in my heart of hearts . . . .
> (3.2.73-75)

3. Citing and punctuating short quotations

If the material being documented is not a long, set-off quotation, the reference is placed before the concluding punctuation mark, which is usually a period.

Example:
The missionaries, unlike the fur traders, subjected the natives to "an institutionalized mode of cultural dismemberment and reconstruction" (LaViolette 18).

Sometimes it is not possible to place a reference at the end of a sentence without confusing the reader about what is being documented. When this is the case, position the reference as closely as possible to the material being documented, preferably at the end of the clause. Note that parenthetical references come **before** punctuation marks.

Example:
One historian refers to "cultural dismemberment" (LaViolette 18), while others use the term "assimilation" (Tobias 39).

4. Citing and punctuating long, set-off quotations

First give the concluding punctuation; then leave a space and give the parenthetical reference.

Example:
The European colonials sought to enforce systematically the acculturation of the natives:

> The casualness of the fur trading type of contacts could no longer be tolerated. Hence, with the arrival of the missionaries and their Christian ethic the task of converting the natives began, and peaceful penetration entered a new phase, based upon an institutionalized mode of cultural dismemberment and reconstruction. (LaViolette 18)

Variations on the Standard Parenthetical Reference

1. If the information normally contained in a reference (author or page number) is clear from your essay's text, the information does not need to be repeated in the parentheses.

   Example:
   Brody draws attention to the emphasis on naming in the language of the Inummariit (134-35).

2. If you are citing an idea that runs through an entire work by an author whose name you have given in the text, you need not include a parenthetical reference at all. The author's name is the only documentation required to enable your reader to find the work in your works cited list (unless there are multiple works by the same author, in which case see 4 below).

   Example:
   Weiler makes the case that sex equity is a complex goal.

3. In many literature and philosophy essays, you make reference to only one text and author throughout. When this is the case, give the author's name only in the first parenthetical citation. The other references will contain only page numbers as it will be clear to the reader who the author is. In addition, if you use one or two other sources sparingly, you can provide full parenthetical citations for those two but continue giving only page numbers for your main source.

4. If you are referring to more than one work by the same author in your essay, include in each reference a shortened version of the title of the relevant work after the author's name. A comma is used to separate the author's name and the title. In the example, reference is being made to Daiches' book *Milton* rather than to another work by Daiches, *Critical Approaches to Literature*, that is also listed in the Works Cited list.

Example:
Milton's prose has been described as "controlled personal feeling expressed through deliberate rhetorical devices" (Daiches, *Milton* 103).

5. When possible, take material from its original source. However, if you are citing a source indirectly (that is, citing a quotation not from where it was originally written but from a text in which it is quoted), put "qtd. in" before the reference to the secondary source.

Example:
Teresa deLauretis notes that micropolitical groups can have an impact through "shifting the 'ground' of a given sign" (qtd. in Weiler 218).

6 Because classic works are available in so many different editions, it is acceptable to provide more information than page number in the parenthetical reference to help readers who have different editions of the same work(s) locate the passages you are documenting. After the page number and a semi-colon, add the necessary information using lowercase abbreviations.

Example:
(16; pt.1, ch.1)

Use this variation only with your professor's consent.

Documenting Online Sources

References in the text
Each in-text citation should refer clearly to a particular entry in the list of works cited, which is at the end of the essay. When citing an entire web page or site, it is sufficient to name its author and title in the text of your paper. If the author is unknown, just mention the title of the web document in your text.

Henry Churchyard's *Jane Austen Information Page* provides a wealth of information on the literature of Regency England.

The Sixties Project is designed to enable those who lived through the sixties to tell their stories to one another and the world.

To cite part of a web page, it is often necessary to give considerable information in the text. An internet document usually does not have numbered pages, so directing the reader to a particular section is made more difficult. Two examples of informative in-text citations follow; one uses a paragraph number to pinpoint a quotation and the other uses a section heading.

> As Ian Buchanan argues, "for Deleuze the effect of pop is conformity" (par. 8).

> In the section of his online biography of Dr. George Rodocanachi entitled "World War II and 'Pat' Line," Long describes how Rodocanachi helped many "soldiers, sailors and airmen escaping from the north before the invading German armies."

or

> An online biography of Dr. George Rodocanachi claims that he helped many "soldiers, sailors and airmen escaping from the north before the invading German armies" (Long, "World War II and 'Pat' Line").

Works Cited

If you are using the parenthetical documentation style A, you must title your list of references "Works Cited." A works cited list contains only works to which there is direct reference in the essay. Works that have been consulted but not cited are not included.

Because the format of the works cited list and the bibliography is identical, follow the guidelines and examples in the "Bibliography" section on pages 74-94.

For ease of reference, a complete "Works Cited" list of all the sources described in the Footnoting/Endnoting and Parenthetical

Documentation Style A (MLA) sections is given here, in alphabetical order.

Bibliography or Works Cited
("Bibliography" if you are using footnoting/endnoting; "Works Cited" if you are using Style A)

"Austria." *Encyclopaedia Britannica Online.* Encyclopaedia Britannica. 3 July 2000 < http://search.eb.com/bol/topic? eu = 117981&sctn = 2 >.

Avison, Margaret. "The Swimmer's Moment." *Winter Sun.* 1962. *Canadian Poetry.* Ed. Ian Lancashire, Sophie Kaszuba, and Sian Meikle. U of Toronto English Library. 8 June 2000 < http://www/library.utoronto.ca/canpoetry/avison/poem7. htm >.

"Axminster Carpets." *Encyclopaedia Britannica: Micropaedia.* 1974.

The Bank of Montreal. *The Centenary of the Bank of Montreal, 1817-1917.* Montreal: Bank of Montreal, 1917.

Belenky, Mary Field, et al. *Women's Ways of Knowing: The Development of Self, Voice, and Mind.* New York: Basic, 1986.

Bettelheim, Bruno. *The Uses of Enchantment: The Meaning and Importance of Fairy Tales.* New York: Borzoi-Knopf, 1976.

Blount, Trevor, ed. *The Personal History of David Copperfield.* By Charles Dickens. Harmondsworth, England: Penguin, 1966.

Bonheur, Rosa. *Plowing Scene.* Museum of Fine Arts, Boston.

Brown, Jonathan. "Karl Muck's Wagner recordings." Online posting. 1 Aug. 2000. 2 Aug. 2000 < news:humanities.music.composers. wagner >.

Brown, Richard Danson. "A 'goodlie bridge' between the Old and the New: the transformation of complaint in Spenser's The Ruines of Time." *Renaissance Forum* 2.1 (1997): 64 pars. 8 June 2000 < http://www.hull.ac.uk/renforum/v2no1/brown.htm >.

Buchanan, Ian. "Deleuze and Pop Music." *Australian Humanities Review* 7 (August-October 1997): 24 pars. 2 June 2000 < http://www.lib.latrobe.edu.au/AHR/archive?Issur-August-1997-buchanan.html >.

Bynum, David E. "Themes of the Young Hero in Serbocroatian Oral Epic Tradition." *PMLA* 83 (1968): 1295-303.

Byrne, David. "The Big Country." *The Talking Heads: More Songs about Buildings and Food.* Sire, 9147-6058, 1978.

Cairns, Julia. "Spry, Constance." *Dictionary of National Biography 1951-1960.* 1971 ed.

Canadian Heritage. *Culture and heritage: Making room for Canada's voices.* Ottawa: Canadian Heritage, 1999. 5 July 2000 < http://www.pch.gc.ca/culture/report/HTM/1.htm >.

Canadian Historical Association. *Regionalism in the Canadian Community 1867-1967.* Ed. Mason Wade. Toronto: U of Toronto P, 1969.

"Capital Punishment." *The Internet Encyclopedia of Philosophy.* Ed. James Fieser and Brad Dowden. U of Tennessee at Martin. 2 June 2000 < http://www.utm.edu/research/iep/c/capitalp.htm >.

Cézanne, Paul. *Still Life with Apples and a Pot of Primroses.* 1890. Metropolitan Museum of Art, New York. 12 July 2000 < http://www.metmuseum.org/collections/images/ep/images/ep51.112.1.R.jpg >.

Chittick, Kathryn. *Dickens and the 1830s.* Cambridge: Cambridge UP, 1990.

Churchyard, Henry. *Jane Austen Information Page.* 8 June 2000 < http://www.pemberley.com/janeinfo/janeinfo.html >.

Cottrell, Robert. "Founding Father." Rev. of *My Six Years with Gorbachev*, by Anatoly S. Chernyaev. *The New York Review of Books* 26 Apr. 2001: 20-22.

Daiches, David. *Critical Approaches to Literature.* Englewood Cliffs, NJ: Prentice-Hall, 1956.

---. *Milton.* New York: Norton Library-Norton, 1966.

Dickens, Charles. *The Personal History of David Copperfield.* Ed. Trevor Blount. Harmondsworth, England: Penguin, 1966.

"Do you know me?" Editorial. *The Globe and Mail* 3 July 2000. 3 July 2000 < http://www.globeandmail.ca/gam/Editorials/20000703/ECELEB.html >.

Dosman, Edgar J. "Hemispheric Relations in the 1980s: A Perspective from Canada." *Journal of Canadian Studies* 19.4 (1984): 42-60.

Early Modern English Dictionaries Database. Ed. Ian Lancashire. Oct. 1999. U of Toronto. 8 June 2000 < http://www.chass.utoronto. ca/english/emed/emedd.html >.

Edison, Aaron. Letter. *Atlantic.* Feb. 2000: 69.

Egoyan, Atom, dir. *The Sweet Hereafter.* Alliance Communications, 1997.

Ehrenpreis, Irvin. *Dean Swift.* London: Methuen, 1983. Vol. 3 of *Swift: The Man, His Works, and the Age.* 3 vols. 1969-83.

Ellin, Abby. "Online Teaching: the Battle in Cyberspace." *New York Times* 6 Aug. 2000. *New York Times Ondisc.* CD-ROM. UMI-Proquest, 2000.

Finley, A.G. *Shipbuilding in St. Martins 1840-1880: A Case Study of Family Enterprise on the Fundy Shore.* M.A. thesis. U of New Brunswick, 1980 Ottawa: Canadian Theses on Microfiche, 1984. 47732.

Fleet, Joan, Fiona Goodchild, and Richard Zajchowski. *Learning for Success: Skills and Strategies for Canadian Students.* Toronto: Harcourt Brace, 1994.

Forth, Christopher E. Rev. of *Leisure Settings: Bourgeois Culture, Medicine and the Spa in Modern France,* by Douglas Peter Mackaman. *H-France, H-Net Reviews* Oct. 1999. 6 June 2000 < http://www/h-net.msu.edu/reviews/showrev.cgi?path=25602 940965000 >.

Franklin, Nancy. "Blarney Stones." Rev. of *Stones in his Pockets,* by Marie Jones. Golden Theatre, New York. *The New Yorker* 16 Apr. 2001: 88-89.

Fulford, Robert. "Regarding Alex Colville." *Saturday Night* 17 June 2000: 30-34.

Gaskell, Elizabeth. "French Life." *The Gaskell Web.* Ed. Mitsuharu Matsuoka. 30 May 2000. Nagoya U, Japan. 8 June 2000 < http://lang.nagoya-u.ac.jp/matsuoka/ EG-Life.html >.

Griffiths, Franklin. "Canada as a Sovereign State." *Canadian Foreign Policy Journal* 2.1 (Spring 1994). Abstract. 3 July 2000 < http://temagami.carleton.ca/npsia/cfpj/fabstracts/fv2.1. html#Griffiths >.

The History of the Book in Canada Project. Ed. Patricia Fleming and Yvan Lamonde. 7 Feb. 2000. U of Toronto Library. 2 June 2000 < http://www.hbic.library.utoronto.ca >.

Holford-Strevens, Leofranc. "Re: Socrates' date of birth and death."
Online posting. 16 Dec. 1999. Classicists. 12 July 2000
<http://listserv.liv.ac.uk/archives/classicists.html>.

Hopkins, Gerard Manley. "The Windhover." *Poems.* 1918.
Representative Poetry On-line. Vers. 2.07. Ed. Ian Lancashire. U
of Toronto. 8 June 2000 <http://www.library.utoronto.ca/
utel/rp/poems/hopkins4.html>.

Human Rights: What to Do about Discrimination or Harassment.
Peterborough, ON: Trent U, n.d.

Hunt, Kevin. "The Cultural Currency of the Book." *CMC Magazine*
Aug. 1998. 1 July 2000 <http://www.december.com/cmc/mag/
1998/aug/hunt.html>.

Keck, Stephen L. "Lady Travellers in the Empire." Online posting. 5
Mar. 1999. H-Albion. 13 July 2000 <http://www2.h-net.msu.
edu/~albion/>.

Kinzer, Stephen. "A Race to Save Roman Splendors From
Drowning." *New York Times on the Web* 3 July 2000. 3 July 2000
<http://www.nytimes.com/library/world/europe/
070300turkey-roman.html>.

"Land of the Eagle." *Nature.* PBS. WNED, Buffalo, NY. 3 May 1992.

LaViolette, Forest E. "The Potlatch Law: Wardship and
Enforcement." *The Struggle for Survival: Indian Cultures and the
Protestant Ethic in British Columbia.* Toronto: U of Toronto P,
1973. 44-97.

Law Society of British Columbia v. Andrews. 1989. 1 S.C.R.

Lawrence of Arabia. Dir. David Lean. DVD. 1962. Columbia Tristar,
2001.

Limbrick, Liddy, et al. *Peer-Power: Using Peer Tutoring to Help Low-
Progress Readers in Primary and Secondary Schools.* Wellington:
New Zealand Council for Educational Research, 1985. 10. ERIC
ED 326 858.

Lindenberger, Herbert. Foreword. *MLA Style Manual and Guide to
Scholarly Publishing.* By Joseph Gibaldi. 2nd ed. New York:
MLA, 1998. xvi-xvii.

Long, Christopher A. Home Page. 8 June 2000 <http://www.users.
dircon.co.uk/~calong/index.html>.

"Making it a Summit for all the Americas." Editorial. *Globe and Mail*
[Toronto] 23 Apr. 2001: A18.

Malcolmson, Patrick, and Richard Myers. *The Canadian Regime.* Peterborough, ON: Broadview P, 1996.

Malo, Jean-Jacques. Rev. of *From Hanoi to Hollywood: The Vietnam War in American Film,* by Linda Dittmar and Gene Michaud. *Viet Nam Generation Journal and Newsletter* 4.1-2 (1992): 12 pars. 2 June 2000 < http://lists.village.virginia.edu/sixties/HTML_docs/Texts/Reviews?Malo_Hanoi_Hollywood.html >.

Manchester, Theresa. Letter. *National Post* [Toronto] 23 Apr. 2001: A15.

May, Nadine. "Re: Conference Paper." E-mail to the author. 11 May 2001.

McCarten, James. "Consider splitting up gasoline retailers and refiners, Ontario task force to tell Ottawa." *CP Online* 3 July 2000. 3 July 2000 < http://www.calgaryplus.ca/cponline/news/ >.

McCarthy, Shawn. "Clock now ticking on free-trade deal." *Globe and Mail* [Toronto] 23 Apr. 2001, metro ed.: A1.

Menander. *Plays and Fragments.* Trans. Norma Miller. London: Penguin, 1987.

Michelangelo. *The Rondanini Pietà.* Museo del Castello Sforzesco, Miilan. *Testament: The Bible as History.* By John Romer. New York: Holt, 1988. Plate 38.

Miller, Norma, trans. *Plays and Fragments.* By Menander. London: Penguin, 1987.

The Millionairess. By Bernard Shaw. Dir. Allen MacInnis. Shaw Festival, Niagara-on-the-Lake. 23 May 2001.

Montgomery, Lucy Maud. *Anne's House of Dreams.* New York: Gosset and Dunlap, 1917. *The Electronic Text Center.* Ed. Jennifer Easley. June 1998. Alderman Lib., U of Virginia. 3 July 2000 < http://etext.lib.virginia.edu/toc/public/MonAnne.html >.

NAC R10. Vol. 1846. 131, 132. "Treaty No. 3 between Her Majesty the Queen and the Saulteaux Tribe of the Ojibbeway Indians at the Northwest Angle of the Lake of the Woods with Adhesions, 3 October 1873."

Neufeld, James, Zailig Pollock, and Suzanne Bailey. Debate. Engl. 205. Trent U, 26 Mar. 2001.

Niero, Christine. "Making Stories: Studies in Contemporary Canadian Metafiction." Diss. Queen's U, 1987.

106

1990 Stoddart Restaurant Guide to Toronto. Toronto: Stoddart, 1990.

Nissan. "Introducing the new Infiniti QX4." Advertisement. *The New Yorker* 24 Apr. 2000: 2-5.

O'Donoghue, Judith A. Personal Interview. 9 Apr. 2001.

Ontario Legislative Assembly. Standing Committee on Social Development. *Report on Food Banks.* 2nd session. 34th Parliament. Toronto: Government of Ontario, May 1983.

Ontario Ministry of Education Home Page. 3 July 2000. Ontario Ministry of Education, Training, Colleges, and Universities. 3 July 2000 <http://www.edu.gov.on.ca/eng/welcome. html>.

Paris, France. Map. US Dept. of State, 1985. 12 July 2000 <http://www.lib.utexas.edu/Libs/PCL/Map_collection/ world_cities/Paris.jpg>.

Phelp, Jenefer. Rev. of *Input, Interaction and the Second Language Learner,* by Susan M. Gass. *Language Awareness* 9 (2000):115-17.

Pratt, Louis H. *Alice Malsenior Walker: an Annotated Bibliography, 1968-1986.* Meckler's Studies and Bibliographies on Black Americans 1. Westport, CT: Meckler, 1988.

Science Study Skills, Section Two: Science Labs. Prod. Ann Wetmore and Christine Shelton. Videotape. Mount Saint Vincent University Student Affairs Dept., 1991.

Shakespeare, William. *Hamlet. William Shakespeare: The Complete Works.* Ed. Alfred Harbage. Baltimore: Penguin, 1969. 930-76.

Sheen, Martin, actor. *The West Wing.* NBC. CTV, Toronto, ON. 25 Apr. 2001.

The Sixties Project. Coordinator Kali Tal. 28 Jan. 1999. Institute for Advanced Technology in the Humanities (IATH), U of Virginia at Charlottesville. 2 June 2000 <http://lists.village.virginia. edu/sixties/ >.

Spector, Phil, prod. *Let It Be.* The Beatles. Apple, SW-6386, 1970.

SSHRC Home Page. 30 June 2000. Social Sciences and Humanities Research Council. 2 July 2000 <http://www.sshrc.ca/english/ index.html>.

Strath, Lucille, Heather Avery, and Karen Taylor. *Notes on the Preparation of Essays in the Arts and Sciences.* 4th ed. Peterborough, ON: Academic Skills Centre, Trent U, 1993.

Swinton, Nelda. "The Inuit Sea Goddess." *Concordia University Art History Theses Abstracts On-line.* Abstract. 3 July 2000

< http://art-history.concordia.ca/RVACanada/abstracts/swinton.html >.

Syrett, John. "Nixon the Great Before Watergate." Hist. 312. Trent U, 7 Mar. 2000.

Taylor, Karen. Online discussion. 1 Aug. 2000. Tapped In. 1 Aug. 2000 < telnet://tappedin.sri.com:7777 >.

Thomas, Susan B. "Concerns About Gifted Children: A Paper and Abstract Bibliography." ERIC, 1974. ERIC ED 091 083.

Time Management for Students. CD-ROM. Toronto: York University, 1999.

Traill, Catharine Parr. *The Backwoods of Canada.* Ed. Michael Peterman. Centre for Editing Early Canadian Texts 11. 1846. Ottawa: Carleton UP, 1997.

Vertigo. Prod. Herbert Coleman and Alfred Hitchcock. Dir. Alfred Hitchcock. Paramount, 1959.

Walker, Mike. "Learning Disabilities: Technology." E-mail to Robert Silvestri. 18 Nov. 2000.

"Wal-Mart heir ousts Gates as world's richest man." *National Post* [Toronto] 23 Apr. 2001: A2.

Weber, Max. *Economy and Society: An Outline of Interpretive Sociology.* Ed. Guenther Roth and Claus Wittich. Trans. Ephraim Fischoff. 3 vols. New York: Bedminster, 1968.

Weiler, Kathleen. "You've Got to Stay There and Fight: Sex Equity, Schooling, and Work." *Changing Education: Women as Radicals and Conservators.* Ed. Joyce Antler and Sari Knopp Bilen. Albany, NY: SUNY P, 1990. 217-36.

Winter, U. "Low marks for history quiz." Letter. *The Globe and Mail* 3 July 2000. 3 July 2000 < http://www.globeandmail.ca/gam/Letters/20000703/MOLETS-4.html >.

WordPerfect Office 2000. Computer Software. Corel Corporation, 1999.

Yeats, W.B. "The Second Coming." *The Norton Anthology of English Literature.* Ed. M.H. Abrams. 5th ed. Vol. 2. New York: Norton, 1986. 1948.

Method Three: Parenthetical Documentation Style B (APA)

This method of documentation is based on the guidelines set by the American Psychological Association (APA). It is used predominantly in **the social and natural sciences** because it allows for greater emphasis on the year in which material has been published. However, within Style B, the punctuation, capitalization, and form of citation in the text and in the list of references vary between disciplines. See Part III-C (pp. 137-62) to discover whether there are any variations from Style B in the discipline in which you are writing.

How to Use Parenthetical Documentation Style B

1. **Summarizing or paraphrasing ideas or information**

a) Whenever you summarize or paraphrase one of your sources and you do not mention the author's name in your sentence, insert in parentheses, next to the item needing documentation, the author's name and the publication date.

   Example:
   A later study showed that this feature was absent in the second group (Woodsworth, 1997).

b) If you mention the author's name in your essay, put only the date in parentheses.

   Example:
   Woodsworth (1997) found that this feature was absent in the second group.

c) A parenthetical citation is not necessary if both name and date appear in the text of your essay.

   Example:
   In 1997, Woodsworth found that this feature was absent in the second group.

2. Quoting or citing a specific part of a source

Although it is usual to give only the author and date of publication when referring to a source, it is sometimes necessary to indicate that the reference is to a specific part of a source, especially statistics, maps, and figures. If you are directly quoting from a source, page references must be added to the name and date. Use "p." for page and "pp." for pages. Even though referring to a part of a source is quite rare in psychology papers, page references must be given for direct quotations:

Examples:
A subsequent experiment showed "no connection between type of settlement and satisfaction" (Vidmar, 1985, p. 139).

Vidmar (1985) found "no connection between type of settlement and satisfaction" (p. 139).

In 1985, Vidmar found "no connection between type of settlement and satisfaction" (p. 139).

3. Citing a work by more than one author

a) If you are citing one work by two authors, give both names always, and use the word "and" to join the names in the text of your essay. But in the parenthetical citation join the names with an ampersand (&).

Examples:
Snyder and Monson (1975) also determined that high self-monitors estimated that they would show more variability across situations in hostility.

An earlier study (Snyder & Monson, 1975) reported that high self-monitors estimated that they would show more variability across situations in generosity and honesty.

b) If you are citing a work by more than two authors and fewer than six, cite all names in the first reference and use the surname of the first author followed by "et al." (meaning "and others") in subsequent references.

Example:
First reference:

One paper (Gergen, Gergen, & Morse, 1972) hypothesizes that religious beliefs affect the use of illegal drugs and alcohol.

Gergen, Gergen, and Morse (1972) studied the correlation between religious beliefs and the use of illegal drugs and alcohol.

Subsequent references:

The relevance of religious beliefs to premarital sex has also been investigated (Gergen et al., 1972).

c) If you are citing a work by six authors or more, cite the surname of the first author followed by "et al." unless you are citing two references that would be shortened to the same form. In this case, cite as many authors as necessary to distinguish between the two references.

Examples:
(Gittelman-Klein et al., 1980)

(Gittelman-Klein, Abikoff et al., 1980)

4. **Citing a corporate author**

Give the full name and and the abbreviation in the first citation; subsequent citations will need only the abbreviation.

Example:
First reference:

(Canadian Psychological Association [CPA], 1991)

Subsequent references:

(CPA, 1991)

5. **Citing a source with no author or with an anonymous author**

a) If you are citing a source with no author, cite the first two or three words of the title in place of the author's name. Use double quotation marks when citing the title of an article or chapter and italicize the title of a book, pamphlet, or periodical.

   Example:
   ("Feminist feedback," 1992)

b) If you are citing a source with an author designated as anonymous, put "Anonymous" in place of the author's name.

   Example:
   (Anonymous, 1993)

6. **Citing different works with the same author and date**

   Use the suffixes a, b, c, etc. to distinguish between the works. In the example, there are two works by Cantwell published in 1978. The suffixes correspond to the entries in the list of references.

   Example:
   (Cantwell, 1978a)
   (Cantwell, 1978b)

7. **Multiple citations in one reference**

a) If you are citing ideas that are expressed in several sources list the citations in alphabetical order by authors' last name and separate them with a semicolon.

Example:
(Rawson, 1986; Shepherd, 1980; Torgesen & Dice, 1980)

b) If you are citing more than one publication of an author, list the dates in chronological order.

Example:
(Wong, 1979, 1986, 1987)

c) If you are citing the same author(s) of several works, some of which have the same publication date, arrange the dates chronologically first and then according to the suffixes a, b, c, etc.

Example:
(Stanovich, 1980, 1983a, 1983b, 1986)

d) If you are citing several works of different authors, arrange the authors in alphabetical order, and, within that alphabetical arrangement, arrange chronologically. Note that the order of authors' names on the cover or title page is not changed; in the example, Mooney is alphabetically before Stanovich, but the order of Mooney and Cole is not changed.

Example:
(Mooney & Cole, 2000; Stanovich, 1983a, 1983b)

8. **Citing a source you have not read**

If you refer to something that you have found quoted or cited in another work, your citation must show this. If, for example, you read about McKinney's findings in an article by Johnson, it would be incorrect to cite in the following manner: (McKinney, 1983). This misleads your reader into believing that you have read or seen the McKinney article in its entirety. Your citation must show that you read *about* McKinney, not that you *read* McKinney. Follow the examples below.

Examples:
(McKinney, 1983, as cited in Johnson, 1988, p. 81)

(Wicker, 1969, as quoted in Zanna, Olson, & Fazio, 1980, p. 107)

References List

In Style B, the list of works cited is titled "References."

Each discipline that uses Style B (APA) has its own particular format for entries in the list of references. Therefore, unless you are writing a paper for psychology, first **check your subject's requirements in Part III-C (pp. 137-62)**. The following information is a guide only, and you may have to modify your entries depending on your discipline.

Guidelines

- All the sources cited in the text must appear in the list of references at the end of the essay. The only exceptions are personal communications such as letters or informal electronic communication, because the list includes only "recoverable" sources.

- The "References" list is paginated continuously with your essay text. If your essay ends on page 8, begin the list on page 9. Appendices appear after the list of references.

- Entries are arranged alphabetically by author's last name. Last names are always listed before first names, which are represented by initials.

- Double-space between and within entries. Use a hanging indent, i.e., the first line is flushed to the left margin while subsequent lines are indented five spaces

- The first word in titles of books and articles, and the first word after a colon, is capitalized, but the other words are not, unless they are proper nouns.

- If there is more than one author, list all the authors' names in the reference list, last name first. The authors' names should be listed in the order in which they appear on the cover page or title page of the source.

- If two or more works by the same author(s) have been used, list them chronologically by year of publication; if they were published in the same year, arrange them alphabetically by title and distinguish each by the addition of a letter suffix to the date (e.g., 1998a, 1998b).

- When arranging several works by the same first author, single-author entries precede multiple-author entries. Multiple-author entries with the same first author and different subsequent authors are arranged alphabetically.

Reference Entries: Examples
Following are two sample entries, one for a book and one for an article in a periodical.

Sample Entry: Book

Dion, S. (1999). *Straight talk: Speeches and writing on Canadian unity.* Montreal: McGill-Queen's University Press.

Sample Entry: Article in a Journal

Edwards, V., Monaghan, F., & Knight, J. (2000). Books, pictures and conversations: Using bilingual multimedia storybooks to develop language awareness. *Language Awareness, 9,* 135-146.

Citations can come from many different kinds of sources. **Find and follow the examples which most closely conform to the sources with which you are dealing. Remember, all types of entries conform to the basic patterns exemplified above.**

References

Books and sections of books

a) **A book by a single author**

Dion, S. (1999). *Straight talk: Speeches and writing on Canadian unity.* Montreal: McGill-Queen's University Press.

b) **A book by two or more authors**

Luthans, F., & Kreitner, R. (1985). *Organizational behavior: Modification and beyond.* Glenview, IL: Scott, Foresman.

c) **A book by a corporate author**

Canadian Psychological Association. (1971). *The future of Canadian psychology.* Ottawa: Science Council of Canada.

d) **A book with an editor or editors**

Fishbein, M. (Ed.). (1967). *Readings in attitude theory and measurement.* New York: Wiley.

Potter, D. S., & Mattingly, D. J. (Eds.). (1999). *Life, death, and entertainment in the Roman Empire.* Ann Arbor: University of Michigan Press.

e) **A book with no author or editor**
Resources for persons with special needs. (1991). Peterborough, ON: Trent University Communications Department.

f) **A specific edition or volume**

Katz, E. (1994). *The film encyclopedia* (Rev. ed.). New York:
Harper Collins.

Wren, D. (1979). *The evolution of management thought* (2nd ed.).
New York: Wiley.

Cummings, L., & Straw, B. M. (Eds.). (1981). *Research in
organizational behavior* (Vol. 3). Greenwich, CT: JAI Press.

g) **An article or chapter in an edited book**
The author or authors of the article or chapter and the editor or
editors of the book must both be included in the citation. Note that
last names and initials are given for **all** authors and editors, and
that the editors' names are given with initials first and last names
last.

Namkoong, G. (1998). Genetic diversity for forest policy and
management. In F. L. Bunnel & J. F. Johnson (Eds.), *The
living dance: Policy and practices for biodiversity in managed
forests* (pp. 30-44). Vancouver: UBC Press.

h) **A contribution to published proceedings of meetings or
symposia**
The symposium or conference name is capitalized.

Cotman, C. W., & Lynch, G. F. (1988). The neurobiology of
learning and memory. In J. F. Kavanagh & T. J. Truss (Eds.),
Proceedings of the National Conference on Learning Disabilities
(pp. 1-69). Parkton, MD: York Press.

See (c) following for contributions to regularly published
proceedings.

118

Articles in Periodicals

a) **An article by one author in a journal**
There are no quotation marks around the title, and the title and the volume number of the journal are italicized. No issue number is given unless each issue begins on page 1, which is rare.

Walsh, J. J. (1996). Higher technological education in Britain: The case of the Manchester Municipal College of Technology. *Minerva: A review of science, learning, and policy, 34,* 219-257.

b) **An article by more than one author in a journal paginated by issue**
The issue number is in parentheses following the volume number.

Taaffe, R., Maguire, M., & Pringle, I. (1985). The impact of social contexts and educational policy/practice on biliteracy development: Ethnolinguistic minority children in English primary schools in Ottawa and Montreal. *Journal of the CAAL, 18*(2), 85-101.

c) **Contributions to annually published proceedings**

Zabrack, M., & Miller, N. (1972). Group aggression: The effects of friendship ties and anonymity. *Proceedings of the 80th Annual Convention of the American Psychological Association 7,* 211-212.

d) **A magazine article**
The date of publication may include the day, month and/or season. The abbreviation "p." or "pp." is used.

Fischman, J. (1987, February). Type A on trial. *Psychology Today,* pp. 42-50.

e) **A newspaper article**

The full date of publication appears in parentheses and the abbreviation "p." or "pp." is used. Note that discontinuous pages would be indicated "pp. 1, 16, 20," for example.

With an author

Highfield, R. (2001, April 23). Red wine, mysterious but healthy. *National Post*, p. D1.

Without an author

White House stands by Arctic drilling. (2001, April 24). *The Globe and Mail*, p. A10.

f) **An editorial or letter to the editor**

Titled

Bresser, R. (2001, April 23). Youth need a say [Letter to the editor]. *The Globe and Mail*, p. A18.

Lost in California's haze. (2001, April 14-20). [Editorial]. *The Economist*. p. 17.

Untitled

Heale, M. (1991). [Letter to the editor]. *Journal of the History of the Behavioral Sciences*, *27*(1), 76-77.

Woolfe, R. (2001, April 14-20). [Letter to the editor]. *The Economist*, p. 8.

g) **Review**

Follow these examples for placement of the title and the type of review, which goes in square brackets. The form of the rest of the entry will depend on what kind of periodical the review is published in. (See examples for periodical entries above.)

Titled

Appiah, K. A. (2001, April 26). Equality of what? [Review of the
book *Sovereign victor: The theory and practice of equality*]. *The
New York Review of Books*, pp. 63-68.

Untitled

Katz, S. (2001, February). [Review of *The languages of Edison's
light*]. *CCC, 52*, 468-470.

h) **A published interview**
These follow the same conventions as reviews. Other conventions
are dictated by the type of periodical in which the interview is
published.

Titled

Lipstein, O. (1992, May/June). Yesterday, today, and tomorrow
[Interview with Nicholas Charney, founder of *Psychology
Today*]. *Psychology Today*, pp. 20, 31.

Untitled

Dettmer, P. (1991). [Interview with Peter D. Rosenstein]. *Gifted
Child Quarterly, 35*, 179-181.

i) **An abstract**
In the example, the first date is the publication date of the abstract;
the second is the publication date of the collection in which it is
found. Both are cited when the two dates differ.

Day, M. C. (1980/1981). Selective attention by children and
adults to pictures specified by color. *Journal of Experimental
Child Psychology, 30*, 277-289. (From *Psychological Abstracts*,
1981, *65*, Abstract No. 1024)

Other Sources

a) **Government documents**

With a person as author

Allen, G. P. (1979). *Days to remember: Observances of significance in our multicultural society.* Toronto: Ontario Ministry of Culture and Recreation.

With a government body as author

Ontario. Ministry of Education. (1980). *Race, religion, and culture in Ontario school materials: Suggestions for authors and publishers.* Toronto: Queen's Printer for Ontario.

b) **Dissertations and theses**

Doctoral dissertation not abstracted in *Dissertation Abstracts International*

Gardner, R. C. (1960). *Motivational variables in second-language acquisition.* Unpublished doctoral dissertation, McGill University, Montreal.

Master's thesis not abstracted in *Masters Abstracts*

Sheppard, A. (1980) *Monologue and dialogue speech of language-impaired children in clinic and home settings: Semantic, conversational and syntactic characteristics.* Unpublished master's thesis, University of Western Ontario, London, ON.

Doctoral dissertation obtained from the university and abstracted in *Dissertation Abstracts International*
The last number is the abstract number.

Hudson, S. A. (1986). Context and children's writing (Doctoral dissertation, University of Georgia, 1985). *Dissertation Abstracts International, 45,* 1669A.

Doctoral dissertation or master's thesis abstracted in either *Dissertation Abstracts International* or *Masters Abstracts* and obtained on university microfilm
The microfilm number is not a necessary part of the reference entry.

Powell, D. A. (1996). Applying risk communication theory to the Canadian agrifood sector. *Dissertation Abstracts International, 57,* 3459B-3551B. (University Microfilms No. 3476B)

c) **Film**

Martin, K. (Producer), & Nash, T. (Director). (1995). *Who's counting?: Sex, lies and global economics* [Film]. (Available from National Film Board of Canada)

d) **Sound recording**
Give a number for a recording after the medium if this number is needed for identification and retrieval. Use parentheses around the medium and the number when a number is necessary. If you do not use a number, use square brackets around the medium.

Jones, J. F. (Speaker). (1992). *Theories of language acquisition* (Cassette Recording No. 5941). Toronto: Association for Bilingualism.

Byrne, D. (Lyricist). (1978). *The Talking Heads: More songs about buildings and food* [Sound Recording]. New York: Sire.

e) **Videotape**

Wetmore, A. (Producer), & Shelton, C. (Producer). (1991). *Science study skills, section two: Science labs* [Videotape]. Halifax, NS: Mount Saint Vincent University Student Affairs Department.

f) **Work of art**

Bonheur, R. (Artist). (1853). *Horse market* [Painting]. New York: Metropolitan Museum.

Documenting Online Sources

The principles of documentation already outlined for Style B apply also to citing sources from the Internet. Following are specific examples of documenting online sources using Style B.

Examples:
According to Kenyon (2000), many famous and creative people have suffered from depression, including Beethoven, Van Gogh, and Robert Louis Stevenson.

Many famous and creative people have suffered from depression, including Beethoven, Van Gogh, and Robert Louis Stevenson (Kenyon, 2000).

Here is the way this web document would be listed in the "References" section at the back of your paper:

Kenyon, C. A. P. (2000). PSY128: Depression. In *Salmon: Study and Learning Materials On-line*. Plymouth, UK: Department of Psychology, University of Plymouth. Retrieved July 4, 2000 from the World Wide Web: http://salmon.psy.plym. ac.uk/year1/DEPRESsion.HTM

When you are quoting or referring to a specific section of an internet document that does not have page numbers, use paragraph numbers or other internal divisions inherent in the document to show your reader exactly where the cited material comes from.

> In the fall of 1913, Carl Jung had terrible dreams about a flood engulfing Europe: "He saw thousands of people drowning and civilization crumbling. Then, the waters turned into blood" (Boeree, 1997, par. 3).

> Boeree (1997) describes Jung's view of an archetype as "an unlearned tendency to experience things in a certain way" (*Archetypes*).

In the "References" section of your paper, the entry for these in-text citations would look like this:

> Boeree, C. George. (1997). Carl Jung, 1875-1961. In *Personality Theories*. Retrieved July 4, 2000 from the World Wide Web: http://www.ship.edu/~cgboeree/jung.html

References

Remember that one of the purposes of citing your sources is to enable a reader to find those sources. Where possible, when you are citing an online document, especially a web page, you should try to ensure that your reference contains the author's name, the date of publication on the Web (if it's available—otherwise indicate it as "n. d."), the title of the document, the title of the web page or other larger work to which it belongs, its URL, and the date on which you accessed it.

The anatomy of a typical internet citation using APA style is given in the following box.

> **Author's Name. (Date of Internet Publication).** *Document Title.* **Date of retrieval statement: Internet Address**
>
> Flintstone, F. (1998, Jan. 4). *Bedrock Ballads.* Retrieved July 21, 2000 from the World Wide Web: http://www. bedrocku/fflintstone/ballads.html

a) **Complete online scholarly projects, reference databases, or professional or personal web sites**

To cite a complete web site (but not a specific page, section, or document on that site), just name the site in the text of your paper and give the site's full URL in a parenthetical citation:

> The *Theory Into Practice (TIP) Database Version 2.0,* created by Greg Kearsley of George Washington University, describes 50 theories relevant to human learning and instruction (http://www.gwu.edu/ ~tip/index.html).

> The American Psychological Association home page provides access points for psychologists and educators, for the public and the media, and for students (http://www.apa.org/).

> Richard Saffran, the father of a school-aged child who is recovering from autism, offers parents a collection of internet and other resources about the use of applied behaviour analysis (ABA) in the treatment of autism, Asperger's Syndrome, or hyperlexia (http://members.tripod.com/ ~RSaffran/aba.html#introduction).

b) **A document, section, or page within a scholarly project, database, or site**

Kenyon, C.A.P. (2000). PSY128: Depression. In *Salmon: Study and Learning Materials On-line*. Plymouth, UK: Department of Psychology, University of Plymouth. Retrieved July 4, 2000 from the World Wide Web: http://salmon.psy.plym. ac.uk/year1/DEPRESsion. HTM

Boeree, C. G. (1997). Carl Jung, 1875-1961. In *Personality Theories*. Retrieved July 4, 2000 from the World Wide Web: http://www.ship.edu/ ~ cgboeree/jung.html

c) **An electronic book**

Baldwin, J. M. (1913). *History of Psychology: A Sketch and an Interpretation*. In Green, C. D. (Ed.), *Classics in the History of Psychology*. Toronto: York University. Retrieved July 5, 2000 from the World Wide Web: http://www.yorku.ca/ dept/psych/classics/ Baldwin/History/

d) **An article in a scholarly journal**

Anderson, C. A. & Dill, K. E. (2000). Video games and aggressive thoughts, feelings, and behavior in the laboratory and in life. *Journal of Personality and Social Psychology, 78*, 772-790. Retrieved July 5, 2000 from the World Wide Web: http://www.apa.org/journals/psp/psp784772.html

e) **An article in a magazine**

Nichols, M. (2000, Jan. 10). Life's building blocks. *Maclean's Online*. Retrieved July 5, 2000 from the World Wide Web: http://www.macleans.ca/pub-doc/2000/01/10/Cover/ 28980.shtml

f) An article in a newspaper or on a newswire

Talaga, T. (2000, April 28). Research stalks gene for
schizophrenia. *The Toronto Star*. Retrieved July 5, 2000 from
the World Wide Web: http://www.thestar.com/thestar/
editorial/health/20000428NEW03_CI-GENE28.html

Azar, B. (1998, September). Split-second evaluations shape our
moods, actions. *APA Monitor*. Retrieved July 5, 2000 from
the World Wide Web: http://www.apa.org/monitor/
sep98/world.html

Breath test 'can diagnose schizophrenia'. (2000, July 4). In *BBC
News Online*. Retrieved July 4, 2000 from the World Wide
Web: http://news.bbc.co.uk/hi/english/health/newsid_
817000/817869.stm

g) A review

Murray, G. E. (2000, July 2) [Review of the book *Anatomies of
Melancholy*]. *New York Times on the Web*. Retrieved July 4,
2000 from the World Wide Web: http://www.nytimes.
com/books/00/07/02/reviews/000702.02verghet.html

h) An abstract

Balon, R., Franchini, G. R., Freeman, P. S., Hassenfeld, I. N.,
Keshavan, M. S., & Yoder, E. (1999, March). Medical
students' attitudes and views of psychiatry [Abstract].
Academic Psychiatry, 23, 30-36. Retrieved July 5, 2000 from
the World Wide Web: http://ap.psychiatryonline.org/cgi/
content/abstract/23/1/30

Sears, C. R., & Pylyshyn, Z. W. (2000, March). Multiple object
tracking and attentional processing [Abstract]. *Canadian
Journal of Experimental Psychology, 54*, (1). Retrieved July 5,

128

2000 from the World Wide Web: http://www.cpa.ca/
cjep/cjep541.html#article1

i) An editorial

Below the belt [Editorial]. (2000, July 5). *Calgary Herald*.
Retrieved July 5, 2000 from the World Wide Web:
http://www.calgaryherald.com/opinion/stories/000705/43
94264.html

j) A letter to the editor

Page, N. (2000, May 20) Offensive behaviour [Letter to the
Editor]. *The Times*. Retrieved July 5, 2000 from the World
Wide Web: http://www.the-times.co.uk/news/pages/tim/
2000/05/20/timopnolt01002.html

k) A government document

Lajeunesse, T., & Jefferson, C. (1998). *Cross gender monitoring
project: First annual report*. Ottawa: Correctional Service of
Canada. Retrieved July 5, 2000 from the World Wide Web:
http://www.csc-scc.gc.ca/text/prgrm/fsw/gender/toce.
shtml

l) A previously published document on the web

Akman, V. (1997). Context as a Social Construct. In Sasa Buvac
& Lucja Iwanska (Eds.) *AAAI-97 Fall Symposium on Context
in Knowledge Representation and Natural Language*,
November 8-10. 1-6. Cambridge, MA. Menlo Park,
California: The AAAI Press. In *Cognitive Science Eprint
Archive*. Retrieved July 4, 2000 from the World Wide Web:
http://cogprints.soton.ac.uk/view_eprint/comp/199806030
/ps/context.ps

m) **A photograph or graphic**

Stanford White Swinging Reaction Time Apparatus
[Photograph] (n.d.) In *Barnard College Psychology
Department History of Psychology Collection.* New York,
Columbia University. Retrieved July 4, 2000 from the
World Wide Web: http://www.columbia.edu/
barnard/psych/museum/b_swing1.gif

n) **A web discussion posting**

Herman. (2000, July 20). Trauma and archetypes. Retrieved Aug.
3, 2000 from Jung Page Forums: http://www.cgjungpage.
org/ubb/Forum2/HTML/000011.html

o) **A listserv message**

Collier, B. (1999, Apr. 28). Political stress theory — an idea for
the group's consideration. Retrieved Aug. 1, 2000 from the
listserv: http://www.mailbase.ac.uk/lists-p-t/social-theory/
1999-04/0083.html

p) **A newsgroup message**

Packer, L. (1998, July 29). Re: Hypnosis and psychosis. Retrieved
Aug. 3, 2000 from the newsgroup:sci.psychology.
psychotherapy

q) **A real-time communication**

Taylor, K. (2000, Aug. 1). Online discussion. Retrieved Aug. 1,
2000 from Tapped In: telnet://tappedin. sri.com:7777

130

Method Four: Number-Reference (CBE)

This method of documentation is used in the **medical sciences, chemistry, computer science, mathematics,** and **physics**, although use of parenthetical documentation (usually a form of Style B) is also acceptable in most of these disciplines (refer to Part III-C). There is no single model of the number-reference method. To give you a **general understanding** of this method, however, we have used the form recommended by the Council of Biology Editors in *Scientific Style and Format: The CBE Manual for Authors, Editors, and Publishers*, 6th edition.

For information on the various forms of the number-reference method acceptable in chemistry, computer science, mathematics, and physics, consult Part III-C.

How to use the Number-Reference Method

In the number-reference method, you insert numbers in your essay's text which correspond to the numbered sources listed at the end of the paper. According to CBE format, entries in the list of references can be arranged in one of three ways, depending on your discipline's preferences. In the first two versions, all entries are assigned a number, and these numbers, rather than the names of authors, are placed in parentheses or superscript within the text when a source is being cited. References are listed either (1) in sequence according to the first reference to each source in the text (see Sample One) or (2) alphabetically by author (see Sample Two).

In the third version, authors' names and the year of publication are placed in parentheses in the text, and references are listed alphabetically by author (see Sample Three).

In all samples, the titles of journals in the list of references are abbreviated in the form given in *CASSI* or in *Serial Sources for the BIOSIS Data Base*.

132

Sample One

Citations in the body of the paper:

Contrary to popular belief, cancer cells do not grow faster than normal cells (1). This erroneous conception may have its origins in the fact that when a cancer cell divides, both daughter cells retain their capacity to divide and are free from normal control mechanisms (2). The state at which this growth occurs is often called the tumour initiation phase (1,3). This stage may be followed by the tumour protection phase and the selection phase. However, the first step toward tumour growth, initiation, does not necessarily lead to cancer; if the second step (promotion) fails to take place, the latent tumour cell will not be attained (2). In fact, "interruption of the metastatic cascade at any of these steps can prevent the production of clinically symptomatic metastasis" (4, p.99).

(Note that in the final citation, a page reference is also needed because a direct quotation is used.)

Entries in the list of references:

1. Doll R, Peto R. The causes of cancer: quantitative estimates of avoidable risks of cancer in the United States today. New York: Oxford University Press; 1981.

2. Rather LJ. The genesis of cancer: a study in the history of ideas. Baltimore: Johns Hopkins University Press; 1978.

3. Friedewald WF, Rous P. The initiating and promoting elements in tumour production. J. Exper. Med. 80: 101-125; 1944.

4. Liotta LA, Stetler-Stevenson WG. Principles of molecular cell biology of cancer: cancer metastasis. In: DeVita VT, Hellman S, Rosenberg SA, editors. Cancer: principles and practice of oncology. 3rd ed. Vol 1. Philadelphia: JB Lippincott Company; 1989: p 98-115.

Sample Two

Citations in the body of the paper:

Contrary to popular belief, cancer cells do not grow faster than normal cells (1). This erroneous conception may have its origins in the fact that when a cancer cell divides, both daughter cells retain their capacity to divide and are free from normal control mechanisms (4). The state at which this growth occurs is often called the tumour initiation phase (1,2). This stage may be followed by the tumour protection phase and the selection phase. However, the first step toward tumour growth, initiation, does not necessarily lead to cancer; if the second step (promotion) fails to take place, the latent tumour cell will not be attained (4). In fact, "interruption of the metastatic cascade at any of these steps can prevent the production of clinically symptomatic metastasis" (3, p.99).

(Note that in the final citation, a page reference is also needed because a direct quotation is used.)

Entries in the list of references:

1. Doll R, Peto R. The causes of cancer: quantitative estimates of avoidable risks of cancer in the United States today. New York: Oxford University Press; 1981.

2. Friedewald WF, Rous P. The initiating and promoting elements in tumour production. J. Exper. Med. 80: 101-125; 1944.

3. Liotta LA, Stetler-Stevenson WG. Principles of molecular cell biology of cancer: cancer metastasis. In: DeVita VT, Hellman S, Rosenberg SA, editors. Cancer: principles and practice of oncology. 3rd ed. Vol 1. Philadelphia: J.B. Lippincott Company; 1989: p 98-115.

4. Rather LJ. The genesis of cancer: a study in the history of ideas. Baltimore: Johns Hopkins University Press; 1978.

134

Sample Three

Contrary to popular belief, cancer cells do not grow faster than normal cells (Doll and Peto 1981). This erroneous conception may have its origins in the fact that when a cancer cell divides, both daughter cells retain their capacity to divide and are free from normal control mechanisms (Rather 1978). The state at which this growth occurs is often called the tumour initiation phase (Doll and Peto 1981; Friedewald and Rous 1944). This stage may be followed by the tumour protection phase and the selection phase. However, the first step toward tumour growth, initiation, does not necessarily lead to cancer; if the second step (promotion) fails to take place, the latent tumour cell will not be attained (Rather 1978). In fact, "interruption of the metastatic cascade at any of these steps can prevent the production of clinically symptomatic metastasis" (Liotta and Stetler-Stevenson 1989, p.99).

(Note that in the final citation, a page reference is also needed because a direct quotation is used.)

Entries in the list of references:

Doll R, Peto R. 1981.The causes of cancer: quantitative estimates of avoidable risks of cancer in the United States today. New York: Oxford University Press.

Friedewald WF, Rous P. 1944. The initiating and promoting elements in tumour production. J. Exper. Med. 80: 101-125.

Liotta LA, Stetler-Stevenson WG. 1989. Principles of molecular cell biology of cancer: cancer metastasis. In: DeVita VT, Hellman S, Rosenberg SA, editors. Cancer: principles and practice of oncology. 3rd ed. Vol 1. Philadelphia: J.B. Lippincott Company. p 98-115.

Rather LJ. 1978. The genesis of cancer: a study in the history of ideas. Baltimore: Johns Hopkins University Press; 1978.

Documenting Online Sources

In-text Citation
When reference is made to a document in the text, the number of the document appears in parentheses. Where a printed document is quoted, its reference number is accompanied by the page number indicating the location of the quotation; this is not generally possible with online documentation and it is therefore important to try to provide as much information about the quotation as possible. The following example gives not only the reference number, but also blends into the sentence the name of the astronomer and the name of the online journal from which the quotation was taken.

> Recent reports indicate that astronomers may have located an extrasolar planet; astronomer Susan Tereby told the online journal *Space Views* that the object's existence may "be telling us gas giant planets are easy to build...." (1)

References

a) **An individual author or authors**

1. Kappe OC, Padwa A. 1996. Furo [3,4-b]indoles and thieno[2,3-c]furans via a Pummerer induced cyclization reaction. < http://www.ch.ic.ac.uk/ectoc/echet96/papers/016/index.htm > Accessed 1998 June 1.

b) **An article**

2. Boatright JH, Gross EA, People JW, Nickerson JM. 1998. An Inexpensive low-temperature incubator. World Wide Web Journal of Biology 3. < http://express.com/w3jbio/vol3.htm > Accessed 1998 April 24.

c) **A previous or simultaneous publication**
Some articles are published on the Web after or at the same time as they are published in print journals or magazines: note that if page numbers are given for the print version, they should also be

included in the citation. In the following example, the article appeared on two separate pages of the printed edition (1 and 7) at the same time as it was published on the Web.

3. Lewis R. 1998. Classic technique reveals HIV in action. The scientist 12(14): 1,7. < http://www.the-scientist. library.upenn.edu/yr1998/July/lewis_p1_980706.html > Accessed 1998 July 7.

d) **E-mail messages and newsgroup postings**

4. Thomas L. < lthomas@nejm.org > 1998 Jan. 30. Rethinking the lives of cells. [Personal e-mail]. Accessed 1998 Feb. 1.

5. Kirk J. < jtkirk@starfleet.gov > 1998 April 1. Is warp speed possible? < alt.science.future > Accessed 1998 April 4.

Currently, the sixth edition of *Scientific Style and Format: The CBE Manual for Authors, Editors, and Publishers* is the most recent, and it provides the guidelines for the number-reference method outlined here. Unfortunately, this edition was published in 1994, so it gives only limited information concerning documenting internet sources. As a result, this section of the book offers few models. To cite other types of web documents using the number-reference method, you must extrapolate from the information provided here and in earlier sections of this book (in particular, Parenthetical Documentation Style B). Another useful tip is to consider the way electronic sources are documented in current scientific journals or to check the current online documentation style guide in an online journal or on a reputable publisher's web site.

PART III
C. PREFERRED DOCUMENTATION METHODS BY
ACADEMIC DISCIPLINE

The list below indicates which documentation method each discipline prefers. Specific examples are given only where the style of documentation differs in some respect from the styles outlined in Part III-B. The examples given always include a published book, an article in a book, and an article in a journal; sometimes, other examples (such as Internet citations) are given, but you are expected to adapt other types of entry to the format illustrated.

If you require further information, consult your instructor or a leading journal in the field. Some journals that you might want to consult are also listed; most journals have online versions listing their preferred documentation style. Because documentation style varies widely across and within disciplines, you are encouraged to check carefully before adopting any particular style, especially in those disciplines whose style guidelines are discussed at great length in this section. The Academic Skills Centre maintains an up-to-date web page with links to the online style guides of major associations and journals (www.trentu.ca/academicskills/style.htm).

Administrative Studies

Any one of the styles of documentation described in this text, as long as it is used correctly and consistently, is acceptable in administrative studies. We suggest that you follow the variation of Style B described in the "Economics" section (pp. 150-51).

Ancient History & Classics

Students should become familiar with the use of *L'Année philologique*. This valuable publications index will help you research your essay, and it will also serve as a style guide to ancient and modern spellings and abbreviations. In addition, consult the *Oxford Classical Dictionary*, third edition (1996), edited by S. Hornblower and A. Spawforth, and *The Cambridge Ancient History*, third edition, edited by N.G.L.

Hammond et al. For essays in classical history, students should consult *Guide to Preparing Essays, Classical History* by K.H. Kinzl. Examine monographs and periodicals in the field to become familiar with common practice in matters of documentation style. Generally, the footnoting/endnoting method is recommended; however, parenthetical documentation is sometimes advised. Follow any guides that accompany your course syllabus. No matter what style you decide to use, use it consistently throughout your essay.

Anthropology/Archaeology

Documentation styles for anthropology and archaeology vary considerably because of the range of sub-disciplines (e.g., ethnography, physical anthropology, etc.) that are included in these disciplines. Two examples, the first based on the style recommended by the American Anthropological Association (AAA) and the second based on that of the Society for American Archaeology (SAA), are modelled in this section. Regardless of the style chosen, students should modify parenthetical documentation Style B in the following ways.

References in the Text
- Commas are eliminated between the elements of the parenthetical citation.
- A colon is used in place of "p." when a page reference is given.
- The ampersand (&) is replaced by "and" in references having two authors.
- The abbreviation "et al." is used *only in parenthetical citations* to refer to works having three or more authors.

Remember that all ideas and data taken from others must be acknowledged in either the text of a paper or in a parenthetical citation. However, do not repeat the name(s) of the author(s) or the publication date of an item in a parenthetical citation if either is mentioned in the text of the paper.

References to certain portions of sources

The !Kung elders believe themselves entitled to the necessities of life because they are full members of !Kung society:

> !Kung elders do not see themselves as burdens. . . . They expect others to care for them when they can no longer do so. Entitlement to care is naturalized within the culture. Elders do not have to negotiate care as if it were a favor; rather it is perceived as a right. (Rosenberg 1990:29)

This is what Ingold calls a "different kind of sociality" (1990:130-31).

The earliest recorded reference to BaMbuti is in a record of an expedition sent from Egypt in the Fourth Dynasty to discover the source of the Nile (Turnbull 1961:15).

References to whole sources

I will compare Salisbury's 1966 study of myth creation in New Guinea with Mead's *Growing up in New Guinea*, published in 1930.

Headland and Reid (1989) investigate the relations between hunter-gatherers and their neighbors, and Hawkes et al. (1982) study the Ache of Eastern Paraguay to discover why hunters gather.

In the 1980s, indigenous peoples spoke to the public directly in various settings, including the courts (Sterritt 1989; People of 'Ksan 1980; Gisday Wa and Delgum Uukw 1989).

List of References

The list of references is usually entitled "References Cited" and includes only those items referred to in the body of the paper. This list follows parenthetical Style B but contains important differences in punctuation and physical layout. Consult your instructor to find out what style she or he prefers.

140

Anthropology

In most areas of anthropology, titles of books and journals are not italicized.

References Cited

Headland, Tom, and Lawrence Reid
  1989 Hunter Gatherers and Their Neighbors from Prehistory
    to the Present. Current Anthropology 30: 43-66.

Ingold, Tim
  1986a The Appropriation of Nature: Essays on Human
    Ecology and Social Relations. Manchester: Manchester
    University Press.

  1986b Evolution and Social Life. Cambridge: Cambridge
    University Press.

  1990 *Comment on* "Foragers, Genuine or Spurious: Situating
    the Kalahari San in History," by J. Solway and R. Lee. Current
    Anthropology 31:130-31.

Marcus, Joyce
  1998 Women's Ritual in Formative Oaxaca: Figurine-Making,
    Divination, Death, and the Ancestors. Ann Arbor: Michigan
    University Press.

People of 'Ksan
  1980 Gathering What the Great Nature Provided: Food
    Traditions of the Gitskan. Vancouver: Douglas and McIntyre.

Rosenberg, Harriet G.
  1990 Complaint Discourse, Aging, and Caregiving among the
    !Kung San of Botswana. *In* The Cultural Context of Aging. Jay
    Sokolovsky, ed. pp. 19-41. New York: Bergin and Garvey.

Sponsel, Leslie S., ed.
  1995 Indigenous Peoples and the Future of Amazonia: An
      Ecological Anthropology of an Endangered World. Tucson:
      University of Arizona Press.

Windes, T.C.
  1999 Chacoan Chronology. Electronic document. http://www.
      colorado.edu/conferences/chaco/chronology.htm

Archaeology

Notice the differences between this style and the one modelled above:
initials are used instead of authors' full first names; book and journal
titles are italicized; and the publisher and place of publication are
reversed and separated by a comma, not a colon.

References Cited

Headland, T., and L. Reid
  1989 Hunter Gatherers and Their Neighbors from Prehistory
      to the Present. *Current Anthropology* 30:43-66.

Ingold, T.
  1986a *The Appropriation of Nature: Essays on Human Ecology
      and Social Relations*. Manchester University Press, Manchester.

  1986b *Evolution and Social Life*. Cambridge University Press,
      Cambridge.

  1990 Comment on "Foragers, Genuine or Spurious: Situating
      the Kalahari San in History," by J. Solway and R. Lee. *Current
      Anthropology* 31:130-31.

Marcus, J.
  1998 *Women's Ritual in Formative Oaxaca: Figurine-Making,
      Divination, Death, and the Ancestors*. Michigan University Press,
      Ann Arbor.

People of 'Ksan
1980 *Gathering What the Great Nature Provided: Food Traditions of the Gitskan.* Douglas and McIntyre, Vancouver.

Rosenberg, H. G.
1990 Complaint Discourse, Aging, and Caregiving among the !Kung San of Botswana. In *The Cultural Context of Aging,* edited by J. Sokolovsky, pp. 19-41. Bergin and Garvey, New York.

Sponsel, L. S. (editor)
1995 *Indigenous Peoples and the Future of Amazonia: An Ecological Anthropology of an Endangered World.* University of Arizona Press, Tucson.

Windes, T. C.
1999 *Chacoan Chronology.* Electronic document. http://www. colorado.edu/conferences/chaco/chronology.htm

Further details and examples can be found in the guides published in the print or electronic versions of *American Antiquity* (for archaeology papers) or *American Anthropologist* (for other anthropology papers). Other major journals in the field have particular style requirements. For example, *American Ethnologist* follows the AAA style, while the *American Journal of Physical Anthropology* follows a scientific style similar to that recommended by the CBE (see pp. 131-36) .

Biology

Although it is sometimes appropriate to use the form of the number-reference method recommended by the Council of Biology Editors (CBE), usually biology uses a form of parenthetical documentation Style B but modifies that style in various ways. As long as students follow the documentation method required by a reputable Canadian journal in the field, they should find that their papers are acceptable. One such method, based on that used in journals such as the *Canadian Journal of Zoology* and the *Canadian Journal of Botany*, is outlined below. These journals publish their documentation style preferences in the first issue of each volume.

References in the Text

- There is no comma between the name of the author and the date of publication: (Busch 2000).
- When referring to a certain portion of a source (e.g., page, figure, table), separate this reference from the date of publication with a comma: (Thomas 1990, p. 156).
- In references to works having two authors, use "and" rather than an ampersand: (Dustin and Saunders 1990).
- In references to works having more than two authors, use "et al." in the *parenthetical citation*: (McCormick et al. 1987). Do not use "et al." in the list of references cited; write out all the authors' names.

In biology journals, using quotations and, consequently, referring to portions of sources is very rare. However, all ideas and information taken from others must be documented. Also remember that, if you mention the author and the date of publication of your source in the text of your paper, it is not necessary to repeat this information in a parenthetical citation.

References to certain portions of sources

Dreissena populations quickly recover from crashes (Ramcharan et al. 1992, fig. 1).

Thomas cannot believe that there is "something fundamentally unnatural, or intrinsically wrong, or hazardous for the species in the ambition that drives us all to reach a comprehensive understanding of nature, including ourselves" (1990, p. 156).

As early as 1962, Rachel Carson wrote, "Future generations are unlikely to condone our lack of prudent concern for the integrity of the natural world that supports all life" (p. 13).

References to whole sources

Dustin and Saunders' research on the photoperiod and aspects of smolting, published in 1990, acknowledged the work of McCormick et al. that was published in 1987.

Research on snapping turtles (*Chelydra serpentina*) has benefited from the contributions of Galbraith and Brooks (1987a, 1987b, 1989).

In the 1980s, much work on the reproductive physiology of fish involved the study of steroids (Fostier et al. 1983; Scott and Canario 1987).

List of References

Only those sources cited in your paper are included in the list of references, which usually has the heading "References." The list itself follows the order of Style B; however, within entries there are some notable differences:

- There are no parentheses around the date of publication.
- Titles are not italicized.
- Volume numbers of journals are in bold face.
- The publisher is listed before the place of publication.
- Journal titles are abbreviated in the form given in *CASSI* or in *Serial Sources for the BIOSIS Data Base* and the names of genera and species are italicized.

References

Anonymous. 1987. Canadian Forestry Service Management Plan for 1986.

Busch, Robert H. 2000. Salmon country: a history of the Pacific Salmon. Key Porter Books, Toronto.

Canadian Hydrographic Service. 1988. Canadian tide and current tables. Vol. 4. Fisheries and Oceans Canada, Ottawa.

145

Dustin, J., and Saunders, R.L. 1990. The entrainment role of
photoperiod on hypoosmoregulatory and growth-related
aspects of smolting in Atlantic salmon (*Salmo salar*). Can. J.
Zool. **68**: 707-715.

Fay, F.H. 1982. Ecology and biology of the Pacific walrus.
North American Fauna No. 74. U.S. Fish and Wildlife
Service, Washington, D.C.

Fostier, A., Jalabert, B., Billard, R., Breton, B., and Zohar, Y.
1983. The gonadal steroids. *In* Fish physiology, Vol. 9A.
Edited by W.S. Hoar, D.J. Randall, and E.M. Donaldson.
Academic Press, New York. pp. 277-372.

Galbraith, D.A., and Brooks, R.J. 1987a. Survivorship of adult
females in a northern population of common snapping turtles,
Chelydra serpentina. Can. J. Zool. **65**: 1581-1586.

Galbraith, D.A., and Brooks, R.J. 1987b. Addition of annual
growth lines in adult snapping turtles, *Chelydra serpentina*. J.
Herpetol. **21**: 359-363.

Galbraith, D.A., and Brooks, R.J. 1989. Age estimates for
snapping turtles. J. Wildl. Manage. **58**: 502-508.

Parsons, J.L. 1977. Metabolic studies on ringed seals (*Phoca
hispida*). M.Sc. thesis, Department of Pathology, University
of Guelph, Guelph, Ont.

Scott, A.P., and Canario, A.V.M. 1987. Status of oocyte
maturation-inducing steroids in teleosts. *In* Proceedings of
the Third International Symposium on Reproductive
Physiology of Fish, 2-7 August 1987, St. John's, Nfld. *Edited
by* D.R. Idler, L.W. Crim, and J.M. Walsh. Memorial
University, St. John's, Nfld. pp. 224-234.

Whitworth, T.L. 1976. Host and habitat preferences, life
history, pathogenicity, and population regulation in species of

Protocalliphora Hough (Diptera: Calliphoridae). Ph.D.
dissertation, Utah State University, Logan.

Use either the *Canadian Journal of Zoology* or the *Canadian Journal of Botany* as a model for other kinds of reference.

Canadian Studies

In interdisciplinary studies such as Canadian studies, use the documentation method indicated in the course syllabus. If none is given, it is best to follow the documentation method preferred in the discipline that most informs the essay you are writing. For example, in an historical essay, use the footnoting/endnoting method; in an economics essay, the form of Style B described under "Economics" would be appropriate; in an essay based on Canadian literature, you would probably want to choose Style A.

Chemistry

Chemistry usually uses a form of the number-reference method. The following explanation of this form is based on the style recommended by the *Journal of the American Chemical Society*.

References in the Text

For in-text citations, you may use one of two formats: superscript numbers or reference numbers within parentheses.

The purple color of plakinidine A and B varies according to the pH[12] and is reminiscent of hue fluctuations observed for unique polycyclic aromatic alkaloids from sponges,[13,14] tunicates,[15,16] and an anemone[17].

Chemical studies (8-11) indicate that the mechanism leading to the production of high energy ions is not yet finally clear. It is known, however, that high energy ion yields are affected much less by oxygen than low energy ion yields (12).

List of References
In the list of references, labelled "References," entries are arranged in order of in-text citation, not alphabetically. Titles of journal articles are not listed, titles of journals are abbreviated, and titles of both journals and books are italicized. Dates of journals are in boldface, and the volume numbers of journals are italicized.

References

(1) Ioele, M.; Bazzanini, R.; Chatgilialoglu, C.; Mulazzani, Q. G. *J. Am. Chem. Soc.* **2000**, *122*, 1900.

(2) Huheey, J. E. *Inorganic Chemistry: Principles of Structure and Reactivity*, 2nd ed.; Harper and Row: New York, 1978; pp 342-348.

(3) (a) Kessler, H.; Gerke, M.; Griesinger, C. *Angew. Chem. Int. Ed. Engl.* **1988**, *27*, 490. (b) Schoolery, J. N. *J. Nat. Prod.* **1984**, *47*, 226.

Note that the in-text citation for the preceding entry may refer either to (3), (3a), or (3b)

(4) Honig, R. E. *J. Appl. Phys.* **1958**, *29*, 549.

(5) Ayra, S. P. In *Dynamics of Atmospheric Flows: Atmospheric Transport and Diffusion Processes*; Singh, M. P. and Raman, S., Ed.; Computational Mechanics Publications: Southampton, 1998; Chapter 1.

Classics: see Ancient History & Classics

Comparative Development Studies

In comparative development studies, as in other interdisciplinary studies, students should consult their instructor or use the form of documentation preferred in the discipline that most informs their essay. In a comparative development studies paper investigating economic theory or policy, for example, the form of Style B described under the heading "Economics" could be used. Likewise, the appropriate variation of Style B could be used in papers informed by political or anthropological research. If your essay focuses on comparative literature or history, on the other hand, Style A or the footnoting/endnoting method might be best. Most frequently, however, some variation of Style B will be acceptable because economics, political science, and anthropology are the disciplines upon which comparative development studies is primarily based.

Computer Science/Studies

Computer science journals generally use a form of either Style B or the number-reference method.

References in the Text: Style B
The journal *Computational Intelligence: An International Journal* suggests the use of a form of Style B. References are cited in parentheses within the text by authors' last names and years of publication:

> Many studies (Hammond and Simons 1987; Bradley 1989;
> Butler 1992) indicate that the results of Butler (1985) are
> valid and relevant.

List of References: Style B
The list of references appears at the end of the paper and is labelled "References."

References

FANNING, D.W. 1997. IDL Programming Techniques.
  Fanning Software Consulting.

KORF, R. 1993. Real-time heuristic search. Artificial
  Intelligence, **43**(2):189-211.

HAMMOND, J. and C. SIMONS. 1987. The cognate language
  teacher: a teaching package for higher education. *In* The use

of computers in the teaching of language and languages, *Edited by* G. Chesters and N. Gardner. CTISS Publications, pp. 100-107.

References in the Text: Number-Reference Method
When following the number-reference method, use superscript numerals for in-text citations:

Many studies[1-3] indicate that the results of Butler[4] are valid and relevant.

List of References: Number-Reference Method
Arrange and number entries in the list of references, which is usually labelled "Works Cited," according to their first mention in the paper. Journal titles may be abbreviated. Note that, for books, the publisher is listed before the place of publication.

Works Cited

1. Nelson, T. "On the Xandu Project." *Byte 15* (Sept. 1990), 298-99.

2. Korf, R. "Real-time heuristic search." *Artificial Intelligence 43*(2) (1993), 189-211.

3. Fanning, D.W. *IDL Programming Techniques*, Fanning Software Consulting, 1997.

4. Butler, C. *Computers in Linguistics*, Blackwell, Oxford, 1985.

Cultural Studies

In interdisciplinary studies such as cultural studies, it is best to follow the documentation method preferred in the discipline which most informs your essay. In a cultural studies essay focusing on historical material, for example, the footnoting/endnoting method would be appropriate. In a cultural studies paper addressing sociological

150

150

questions, however, the form of Style B used in sociological journals might be preferable.

Economics

Economics uses a form of Style B modified in the following ways and based on the style recommended by the *Canadian Journal of Economics*:

References in the Text
- The abbreviation "p." is eliminated in citations in the text: (Smith 1976, 740).
- An "and" rather than an ampersand (&) is used when referring to sources with two authors: (Arrow and Kurz 1970).
- When citing more than two works by the same author(s) published in the same year, list only the distinguishing lower-case letter after the comma(s): (MacDonald 1988a,b).

In articles published in economics journals, authors' names appear more frequently in the text than in parenthetical citations. Here is an example:

> Using this rate as a social discount rate is recommended in several studies, including Marglin (1963), Feldstein (1964a), Diamond (1968), Kay (1972), Ahsan (1980), and Mendelsohn (1981, 1983).

List of References
- The first names of authors are usually spelled out in full in the list of references, entitled "References."
- The names of second and subsequent authors appear in natural order.
- There is no period after the date of publication, which is placed in parentheses.
- There are quotation marks around the titles of unpublished sources, including dissertations and reports, and of chapters or portions of published sources, as well as around the titles of articles in journals and books.

- No period follows the title of a book, which is italicized.
- The place of publication and the publisher are placed in parentheses.
- No period closes an entry.

Here are some sample entries in the list of references:

References

Demougin, Dominique, and Aloysius Siow (1991) 'Careers in ongoing hierarchies,' unpublished manuscript,University of Toronto

Hill, R. Carter, William E. Griffiths, and George G. Judge (1997) *Undergraduate Econometrics* (New York: Wiley)

MacDonald, Glenn (1988a) 'Job mobility in market equilibrium,' *Review of Economic Studies* 55, 153-68

– (1988b) 'The economics of rising stars,' *American Economic Review* 78, 155-66

Marx, Karl (1857/8) *The Grundrisse.* Text references to R.C. Tucker (1978) *The Marx-Engels Reader*, 2nd ed. (New York: Norton)

Portes, Richard (1997) 'Users and abusers of economic research,' in *Economic Science and Practice: The Roles of Academic Economists and Policy-makers*, ed. Peter A.G. van Bergeijk, A. Lans Bovenberg, Eric E.C. van Damme, and Jarig van Sinderen (Cheltenham: Edward Elgar)

Revenue Canada (1998) 'Revenue Canada confirms dumping of baby food.' http://www.rc.gc.ca/simad1180-p.htm

Smart, Michael (1998) 'Taxation and deadweight loss in a system of intergovernmental transfers,' *Canadian Journal of Economics* 31(1), 189-206

Education

Most frequently, journals in this field require authors to follow the APA format of documentation, which we call Style B.

English Literature

English literature students may use either the footnoting/endnoting method or parenthetical documentation Style A. If the essay focuses on only one text, or on a few texts, Style A is preferable. If, however, the essay relies on a diverse number of sources (particularly secondary sources), the footnoting/endnoting method may be more helpful to the reader.

Environmental and Resource Science/Studies

Environmental science journals usually recommend a form of Style B. The following description of this form is based upon that required by the *Canadian Journal of Fisheries and Aquatic Sciences*. Additional examples are given in the "Biology" section.

References in the Text
- Do not place a comma between the name(s) of the author(s) and the date of publication in parenthetical citations: (Walker 1980).
- References to particular sections or pages of an item are rare in biology or environmental science papers; however, if this information is required, it should be put inside the parenthetical citation in the following way: (Walker 1980, p. 14) or (Jones 1990, fig. 3).
- When referring to an item that has more than two authors, include only the surname of the first author followed by "et al." in either the parenthetical citation or the text of your paper: (Taylor et al. 1991) or Taylor et al. (1991) compared . . . .

List of References

- There are no parentheses around the date of publication.
- Titles are not italicized.
- Volume numbers of journals are in bold face.
- The publisher is listed before the place of publication.
- Journal titles are abbreviated in the form given in *CASSI* or in *Serial Sources for the BIOSIS Data Base* and the names of genera and species are italicized.

References

Addicott, J.F. 1978. Niche relationships among species of aphids feeding on fireweed. Can. J. Zool. **56**: 1837-1851.

Levine, L. 1973. Biology of the gene. C.V. Mosby Co., Saint   Louis.

Ross, A.F. 1966. Systematic effects of local lesion formation. *In* Viruses of plants. *Edited by* H.B.R. Beemster and J. Dijkstra. North-Holland Publ. Co., Amsterdam. pp. 127-150.

StreamNet. 1998. StreamNet database (version 98.3), April 1998 (16 March 1998) (database downloaded todisk). StreamNet, Gladstone, Ore. (URL: http://www.streamnet.org/ accesstable.html).

Geography

Because this discipline deals with the earth and its life, it can be considered either a social or a physical science. Consequently, many different documentation methods are acceptable in geography. In almost all cases, however, the style of referencing is to cite the author's last name and the year of publication in the text. Frequently, geography journals use a form of parenthetical documentation similar to Style B. One variation of Style B, modelled following, is based on the method of documentation required by *The Canadian Geographer*.

154

References in the Text

- The year is separated from the author's last name by a comma, and the abbreviation "p." is not used: (Bourne, 1982, 43).
- In references to works with two authors, an "and" is used rather than an ampersand (&): (Brown and Brown 1983, 111).

List of References

- The list of references, called "References," contains only those works cited in the paper.
- The list of references is arranged in alphabetical order according to the authors' surnames. Multiple entries for a single author are arranged chronologically, by date of publication. If two or more publications by the same author(s) have the same publication date, add the suffixes a, b, c, etc., to differentiate entries.
- The authors' names are in upper case.
- There are no parentheses around the date of publication.
- The titles of articles and portions of books are in quotation marks.
- The place of publication and publisher are enclosed in parentheses.
- No periods separate elements of an entry, and no period closes an entry.

References

BRITTON, J.N.H. 1974 'Environmental adaptation of industrial plants: Service linkages, locational environment and organization' in F.E.I. Hamilton, ed. *Spatial Perspectives on Industrial Organization and Decision Making* (Chichester, Sussex: Wiley) 363-390.

CARTWRIGHT, W., PETERSON, M.P., and GARTNER, G. (eds.) 1999 *Multimedia Cartography* (Berlin/New York: Springer).

HAGGETT, P. 1979 *Geography: A Modern Synthesis* (New York: Harper and Row).

LAWRENCE, E.N. 1965 "Terrestrial climate and the solar cycle" *Weather* 20, 334-343.

History

History uses the footnoting/endnoting method.

Interdisciplinary Studies

In interdisciplinary studies it is best to follow the documentation method preferred in the discipline that most informs the essay. For example, an essay that focuses on sociological themes would use a variant of Style B; a paper on an historical topic would probably require the footnoting/endnoting method.

Mathematics

The form of documentation used in mathematics varies from journal to journal, but it generally follows the number-reference method. Following is a description of the number-reference method recommended by the *Canadian Journal of Mathematics*.

References in the Text
In-text citations should be in square brackets:

> Facially symmetric spaces were introduced [12] and studied in [15]. The results obtained here and in [1], [2], and [5] are consistent.

List of References
Entries in the list of references, entitled "References," are alphabetized and then numbered:

References

1. R. Finn, *Capillary Surface Interfaces*, Not. A. Math. Soc. **46**(1999), 770-781.

156

2. Y. Friedman and B. Russo, *Affine structure of facially symmetric spaces*, Math. Proc. Camb. Philos. Soc. **106**(1981), 107-124.

3. ------, *Some affine geometric aspects of operator algebras*, Pac. J. Math. **137**(1989), 123-144.

4. P. Ney de Souza and J. N. Siwa, *Berkeley Problems in Mathematics*, Springer, Berkeley, 1998.

Modern Languages

Any one of the styles of documentation described in this text, as long as it is used correctly and consistently, is acceptable in modern languages. Parenthetical documentation Style A may be preferable for literature essays that focus on one or a few texts; for essays that have a diverse and large number of secondary sources, the footnoting/endnoting method may be better. The anthropological form of Style B may be most appropriate for linguistics papers.

Native Studies

In native studies both the footnoting/endnoting method and the parenthetical documentation method (Style A or a variation of Style B) are acceptable. Usually, journals in this discipline use a variation of Style B that is similar to that used in anthropology or archaeology journals. This variation, modelled in the *Canadian Journal of Native Studies*, is outlined here.

References in the Text
- A colon is used in place of "p." when a page reference is given: (Badgley, 1980:23).
- When citing a source with two authors, "and" rather than an ampersand (&) is used: (Honigmann and Honigmann, 1953:57).
- If the names of the authors appear in the text, do not repeat them in the parenthetical citation:

This is clear particularly in Powers (1977, 1982, 1986a, and 1986b).

Also do not repeat the publication date of a source if this information appears in the text of your paper:

> As DeMaille and Lavenda wrote in 1977, "The concept of power is a key to understanding the cultural systems of the Siouan peoples of the Plains" (153).

List of References

References

Asch, Michael and P. MacKlem
  1991 Aboriginal Rights and Canadian Sovereignty: An Essay on *R. vs. Sparrow*. *Alberta Law Review* 57:498-517.

Barbeau, Marius
  1960 Huron-Wyandot Traditional Narratives. *National Museum of Canada Bulletin* 165.

Canada. Medical Services Branch, Health Canada
  1997 *First Nations HIV/TB Training Kit*. Ottawa: Medical Services Branch, Health Canada.

Daniel, Richard
  1999 The Spirit of Treaty Eight, pp. 47-100 in Richard T. Price (Editor): *The Spirit of the Alberta Indian Treaties*. 3rd ed. Edmonton: University of Alberta Press.

LaPrairie, C.P.
  1984a Select Socio-Economic and Criminal Justice Data on Native Women. *Canadian Journal of Criminology* 26:161-169.
  1984b Native Women and Crime. *Perceptions* 7(4):25-27.

Nelms, Joyce E.
  1973 *The Indian Woman and Household Structure in Mill Creek, British Columbia*. Unpublished M.A. thesis Department of Anthropology, University of Victoria.

Ridington, Robin
1998 Coyote's Cannon: Sharing Stories with Thomas King.
American Indian Quarterly 22(3):343-362.

Tiller, Veronica E.
1983 Jicarilla Apache, pp. 440-61 in Alfonso Ortiz (Editor):
Handbook of North American Indians. Vol. 10: *Southwest*.
Washington: Smithsonian Institute.

Philosophy

Philosophy students may use either the footnoting/endnoting method or parenthetical documentation Style A. If the essay focuses on only one primary text, or on a few texts, Style A is preferable. If, however, the essay relies on a diverse number of sources (particularly secondary sources), the footnoting/endnoting method may be more appropriate.

Physics

The American Institute of Physics recommends the following form of the number-reference method of documentation.

References in the Text: American Institute of Physics
In the paper, use superscript numerals that correspond to the numbered entries in the list of references:

> Some studied the physical aspects of Milne's theory.[20-26]
> Others raised issues regarding the philosophical aspects of Milne's work.[5,32,40-44]

List of References: American Institute of Physics
Entries in the list of references, called "References," are arranged in order of in-text citation. Note that the volume numbers of journals are in boldface, journal titles are abbreviated, and the titles of journal articles are often not given. For books, italicize titles and provide specific page references.

159

References

1. R. Zallen and M.L. Slade, Phys. Rev. B. **18**, 5775 (1978).

2. F. Herlach, Rep. Prog. Phys. **62**, 859-920 (1999).

3. R.P. Crease and C.C. Mann, *The Second Creation: Makers of the Revolution in Twentieth-Century Physics* (Rutgers, New Brunswick, NJ, 1996), pp. 350-383.

4. N.H. Burnett and G.D. Enright, Can. J. Phys. **64**, 920 (1986).

5. W. Siegel, Phys. Lett. **94B**, 37 (1980); L.V. Audeev and O.V. Tarasov, Phys. Lett. **112B**, 356 (1982); L.V Audeev and A.A. Vladimirov, Nucl. Phys. **B219**, 262 (1983).

References in Text: *Canadian Journal of Physics*
The *Canadian Journal of Physics* requires a slightly different form of the number-reference method. The in-text reference numbers are in square brackets: [6, 7] or [20].

List of References: *Canadian Journal of Physics*
References in the list of references look like this:

References

1. V. Elias, G. Mckeon, and R.B. Mann. Can. J. Phys. **63**, 1498 (1985).

2. J.D. Singh. *In* Mach's principle: From Newton's bucket to quantum gravity. *Edited by* J. Barbour and H. Pfister. Birhauster, Boston. 1995. pp. 9-57.

3. L. Robin. *In* Proceedings of the 4th International Conference on Kinetics, London, June 4-5, 1980. *Edited by* J. Jones. Plenum Press, London. 1981. pp. 98-103.

4. C. Cercignani. Ludwig Boltzmann: The man who trusted atoms. Oxford University Press, Oxford. 1998. pp. 14-38.

Use either the *Canadian Journal of Physics* or the most recent style manual published by the American Institute of Physics to find more information on and models of the two formats described here.

Political Science/Studies

Although both parenthetical documentation and the footnoting/endnoting method are acceptable in political studies, the latter method is recommended by most journals in the discipline, including the *Canadian Journal of Political Science*.

Psychology

Psychology uses Style B. See pages 109-29 for a detailed description of this style, which is based on information from the *Publication Manual of the American Psychological Association*. Use this manual for other kinds of reference.

Sociology

Sociology uses a form of Style B. Students should make the following changes to that style.

References in the Text
- Separate the date of publication and the location reference with a colon: (Hochschild, 1989: 15-17) or (Smith, 1989: Figure 2.3).

List of References
- In the list of references, entitled "References," the titles of books and journals are italicized, and the titles of chapters in books, articles in books, and articles in periodicals are placed in quotation marks.
- If there are two or more authors, list the second and subsequent authors with their first names first and their surnames last in the "References" section.

Pay close attention to the spacing, layout, and punctuation of the following examples:

Banner, David K. and T. Elaine Gagne ̄
 1998   *Designing Effective Organizations: Traditional and
        Transformational Views.* Thousand Oaks, CA: Sage
        Publications.

Bellamy, Leslie and Neil Guppy
 1991   "Opportunities and obstacles for women in Canadian higher
        education." In J. Gaskell and A. McLaren, eds., *Women and
        Education*, 2nd edition, pp. 163-192. Calgary: Detselig.

Gabin, Nancy Felice
 1984   Women Auto Workers and the United Automobile
        Workers' Union (UAW-CIO), 1935-1955.   Unpublished
        Ph.D. dissertation. University of Michigan.

Koch, Dorothea
 1990   Interview, July 26.

Matthews, David Ralph
 1998   "Sociology and its Publics - Whither Sociology? An
        Introduction." *Canadian Journal of Sociology*
        23(2): 135-40.

Psacharopoulos, George, ed.
 1987   *Economics of Education: Research and Studies.* New York:
        Pergamon.

Turner, Jonathan H.
 1975a "A strategy for reformulating the dialectical and functional
        conflict theories." *Social Forces* 53(2):   433-44.
 1975b "Marx and Simmel revisited." *Social Forces* 53(3): 619-27.

Statistics: see Mathematics

Women's Studies

In interdisciplinary studies such as women's studies, it is best to follow the documentation method preferred in the discipline that most informs the essay. For example, in a women's studies essay focusing on historical material, the footnoting/endnoting method would be appropriate; in a women's studies paper addressing sociological questions, the form of Style B used in sociological journals would be best.

APPENDIX 1: ABBREVIATIONS FOR PROVINCES AND STATES

These abbreviations are used in lists of references in all styles. Some disciplines and journals, however, prefer a different method of abbreviation. Consult Part III-C for details.

CANADA

AB	Alberta	NT	Northwest Territories
BC	British Columbia	NU	Nunavut
MB	Manitoba	PE	Prince Edward Island
ON	Ontario	QC	Quebec
NB	New Brunswick	SK	Saskatchewan
NF	Newfoundland	YT	Yukon
NS	Nova Scotia		

UNITED STATES

AL	Alabama	LA	Louisiana
AK	Alaska	ME	Maine
AS	American Samoa	MD	Maryland
AZ	Arizona	MA	Massachusetts
AR	Arkansas	MI	Michigan
CA	California	MN	Minnesota
CZ	Canal Zone	MS	Mississippi
CO	Colorado	MO	Missouri
CT	Connecticut	MT	Montana
DE	Delaware	NE	Nebraska
DC	District of Columbia	NV	Nevada
FL	Florida	NH	New Hampshire
GA	Georgia	NJ	New Jersey
GU	Guam	NM	New Mexico
HI	Hawaii	NY	New York
ID	Idaho	NC	North Carolina
IL	Illinois	ND	North Dakota
IN	Indiana	OH	Ohio
IA	Iowa	OK	Oklahoma
KS	Kansas	OR	Oregon
KY	Kentucky	PA	Pennsylvania

PR	Puerto Rico	VT	Vermont
RI	Rhode Island	VA	Virginia
SC	South Carolina	VI	Virgin Islands
SD	South Dakota	WA	Washington
TN	Tennessee	WV	West Virginia
TX	Texas	WI	Wisconsin
UT	Utah	WY	Wyoming

INDEX

166

172

Notes

Notes

Notes

Notes

Notes

Notes

Notes